Carys Evans-Corrales
Talking
Girl

Carys Evans-Corrales

TALKING Girl

A Memoir

Small Stations Press

Published in 2014 by
SMALL STATIONS PRESS
1-A Jose De San Martin Street, 1111 Sofia, Bulgaria
You can order books and contact the publisher at
www.smallstations.com

Text and photographs © Carys Evans-Corrales, 2014
Design © Yana Levieva, 2014
© Small Stations Press, 2014

The cover photograph shows the author, Carys Evans-Corrales, in Jamaica in 1967. All the photographs in this book have been reproduced with permission from the author's archives. The author wishes to thank the many friends who provided information for this book.

ISBN 978-954-384-025-0
All rights reserved

for Peter and Jenny

CONTENTS

9 ~ Preface

13 ~ **1** CHOOSING SIDES

61 ~ **2** ISLAND GIRL?

101 ~ **3** SPANISH EYES

143 ~ **4** AMERICA: STEP ASIDE, LADY!

LIST OF PHOTOGRAPHS

The author in Jamaica in 1967 (*cover*).

The author's parents' wedding in London in 1946 (*p. 12*).
The author aged one with her amah, Ah Lien, learning Hainanese (*p. 18*).
The author with her dog Tommy (on the left) and Fifo at Petaling Jaya in 1965 (*p. 52*).
The author with her mother and brother at Kuala Lumpur Zoo in 1965 (*p. 53*).
The author at the beach in Jamaica in 1967 (*p. 60*).
The author with her mother and brother in the garden of their haunted house in Kingston in 1968 (*p. 63*).
The author and a neighbor in Kingston in 1968 (*p. 63*).
The author (on the left) with her brother and a friend at Tony's place in Ocho Rios in 1968 (*p. 89*).
The author with friends during her year abroad in Seville (*p. 100*).
The author revisiting the Coira family in Galicia, Spain, in 2005 (*p. 141*).
The author's wedding to Scott Corrales in 1988 (*p. 142*).

Preface

As a schoolgirl in the Kuala Lumpur of 1964, I would walk the twenty minutes from the shady excitement of St Mary's Girls' School to Foch Avenue, the teeming confluence of all bus routes and birthplace of adolescent crushes. The route was varied, leading from a quiet suburban road through leafy residential avenues to the hub of Foch Avenue itself: an exhilarating but familiar visual and auditory explosion of Chinese restaurants, cheongsam shops and sidewalk hawkers, punctuated by odorous bounties of dried fish and squid, kumquats and desiccated plums, all enlivened by mangy stray dogs wandering among outdoor eateries where still thrashing python coils were skinned before the expectant gaze of seated patrons.

It was toward the end of the last of the shady stretches that I caught sight of the sadhu. The reason for his presence at the brink of all that bustle is not clear; it occurs to me only now that he may have lived in one of the tranquil, tree-lined streets beyond. We were, I think, the only two people in sight on that bare urban watershed. In any case, from the glimpse that I caught of him, I saw that he was dark-skinned (perhaps Tamil), large-eyed and pleasantly intelligent-looking. He was also completely naked. Much more unnerving, however, was that he had a thick metal skewer piercing his outstretched tongue and seemed oblivious to it.

One does not stare at people undergoing a religious experience, and especially not at handsome, naked young men on lonely streets, so I averted my eyes and continued on my way, schoolbooks in hand. Suddenly I heard the man's voice materialize within my head.

'Don't be afraid,' it said kindly. 'I won't hurt you.'

I have pondered this incident ever since and have been questioned closely about it. How could the man have addressed me if he had a skewer through his tongue? Was there somebody else around? Hadn't I been terrified at being faced by a naked man on a deserted road? What did I mean, I heard his voice in my head? Maybe it was *my* head that needed looking at. But I knew beyond all doubt that I had heard it.

An English friend recently asked me, 'What sort of an accent did the voice have?' He was answered crossly by others present who saw the question as aggressively unmetaphysical and embarrassingly typical of the age-old British class warfare waged through language. To me, however, the friend's question has always seemed to encapsulate the kernel of the whole mystery.

Malaysian English itself is a territory of infinite inflexions, most of which were very familiar to me. The voice I heard was light, very clear and with a slight Indian accent, much lighter than those I had heard before this. It also displayed an ease with

English that bespoke a high level of education and a sophisticated background. The intonation was enlightened and progressive, but not arch or urbane.

Why should I have perceived any accent at all in a telepathic communication? Shouldn't I have received his good intentions as a kind of wordless knowing of the sort I later came to experience? Had it merely been, after all was said and done, the accent I would have *expected* from such an advanced being? Not in my limited experience of Hindu religious men, who were immersed in their own cultural vibration, free of any taint of colonialist preoccupations. The concept of a European-educated Hindu mystic did not at that time jibe with my short personal experience.

However, the many years and territorial changes that followed this cherished incident have reinforced its main thrust: that I have attended more to the secrets of the voice than to the blessing itself. This book has evolved from the consequences of that absorbing fact. It is also an account of a pilgrimage in search of truth and selfhood through the sounds of words, and a final destination – devoid of the alluring aesthetic of any one particular language – in a seemingly codeless world.

Carys Evans-Corrales
Bradford, Pennsylvania
January 10, 2014

The author's parents' wedding in London in 1946.

1 CHOOSING SIDES

I realize that I have lived my life like a translator, between two languages and in two languages, never quite sure whether the anchors might be the same in both languages. The scream in one language required the breath of a pianissimo in the other language. I have transplanted myself into other cultures, always keenly aware of the fact that the sound of footsteps on the other side of the river, in the new cultural landscape, reverberated in different keys.

Rainer Schulte

One steamy night in 1949, as my mother was soaking in the luxury of a bath brimming with hot water, an astonishing thing happened. A tiny, delicate wall lizard came unstuck from the ceiling and landed smack-plop on her soapy stomach. It was her first night in Singapore, and my mother took the incident as a lucky omen for her family's new life in Southeast Asia. I cannot believe that she had any idea then of what was in store.

My parents had just disembarked with their three-month-old daughter from the P&O liner that had eased them away from the bleakness of postwar London. Married just three years before, they had been living in a one-room flat in Hampstead with my father's old spaniel, Sally, buying secondhand chairs one at a time and bearing them joyfully home on the Tube, happy to be free from the suffocation of family expectations in South Wales. A young Anglo-Saxon scholar and semanticist, my father was teaching foreign languages at a London boys' school when he answered an advertisement for a lecturer in English Literature at the University of Singapore. When my father was offered the job, he and my mother did not hesitate for a second. They left their bomb-scarred but beloved London, to which they had all but eloped at war's end, and took the first boat out. They left behind a life of rationing, of watching how much hot water they could use, of feeding the gas meter with shillings they could ill afford, of sitting in the movies to watch endless continuing sessions of films just to enjoy the free warmth. They had been blissfully happy in spite of all their tribulations, which had included such items as my father receiving the news on their wedding day that the teacher for whom he was to act as a substitute had recovered early from his illness, thus putting my father out of a job. They arranged to spend the early days of their marriage at a friend's flat, but the night after they were married a group of Jewish refugees had shown up and my father had tramped out into the smoggy night to make some extra room for them. My mother told me that her heart broke when she saw him bundled up in a woolen scarf, coughing with bronchitis as he made his way in the damp darkness.

Singapore was ablaze with equatorial sunlight, with a million neon lights, with all the sultry blare of a booming cosmopolitan city. Because of its situation roughly halfway between India and China, the Lion City had for centuries been a vital port of call for traders in silks and spices, and particularly for the Arab merchants who brought their wares from the Middle East. By the time my parents arrived there, Singapore had become a free port, an exploding, multi-hued mosaic of peoples, languages and goods. There were immigrants from wildly different regions of India and China, as well as the Malays, who, though not the original inhabitants of the land, had arrived several centuries earlier. Indonesians of all ethnic groups enriched this human stew, as did the descendants of Dutch and Portuguese settlers, and the British employed in Far East commerce or attached to the colonial administration or the armed forces. Many of these, however, closed themselves off into enclaves and didn't mix socially at all with the local population. When the University of Singapore was founded, my father once told me, someone went out with a big shopping basket and a lot of money and gathered together the best faculty they could get from around the globe. As a result, during the fifties, an extraordinary group of expatriate academics from several countries had gathered in the city, and there was a clear sense of excitement, a feeling that something of importance was taking place. The island had just a few years before been liberated from Japanese occupation and was struggling for its own political identity. It was a thrilling time to be there, and the brilliance of its moment was captured – with varying degrees of success – by a number of English poets and novelists. One of these was Patrick Anderson, a colleague of my father's and an habitué of our living room, who wrote a novel called *Snake Wine*. My parents feature heavily in the book. According to my mother, she and my father were – somewhat to their discomfiture – the only ones of all their many friends who were not portrayed as singularly revolting people. The book didn't fall into my hands until I was well into my teens. When I asked why I hadn't been shown it before, I was informed, 'Well, it isn't terribly good, dear.' I admit that my only reason for reading it at all was sheer vanity: I'd heard from a non-related grown-up that there was a description of me as a toddler in it. Although I had assumed that there was nothing about my parents that I could possibly not know, when I finally did read it I was puzzled by an *in absentia* description of my mother. What was all that about my warm, emphatic, fun-loving mother going through life with 'a certain helpless, almost little-girlish vivacity as though social life were something in which she "dressed up"'? This has remained all these years like a daffodil bulb underground, coming to flower only in the slowly focusing light of my own understanding. In the same passage, my father is described as perhaps being 'still in the process of one of his retreats, during which he constructs those semantic theorems of his and from which he emerges with a passion for nights at the Flying Club interspersed with bouts of Science Fiction'. This was a father I recognized – the author was half right as to my parents. But I was described as having 'staggered pompously into view, a child straight out of the Eighteenth Century, whose pale important face was made quaintly beautiful by a pair of amber-colored eyes'. So far, the passage is reasonably, if not overwhelmingly, flattering. But then the author goes on to say that our amah's beautiful young daughter, the old yellow dog we called Ianto and my good self 'each had the same quality of an independence that could not be trifled with; all were mannered in their different ways – difficult to pat the dog, impossible to cuddle the child'. This curious me-baby then apparently broke the spell and 'called in some foreign language particular to itself'.

My mother danced a little jig of scorn when I read this out to her several years later. 'Unpronounceable Welsh name, indeed!' she snorted. 'The man was a gibbering idiot! Anybody with half a brain can say "Ianto"!' But the truth remains that Anderson painted all three of us – my brother John was to arrive nearly two years later – as each in a separate but imaginary world, protected from the overwhelming banality of 'real life' that one is to assume the author was able to capture elsewhere in the novel. I like to think that my part of the passage, however, describes a one-year-old surveying her linguistic terrain and choosing her battles with language and reality. No wonder I couldn't be cuddled.

But cuddled or not, I got plenty of attention. I have an early photograph of myself in front of our first home in Singapore, in the coincidentally named Evans Flats on Evans Road. I am being held up by an old woman with her hair smoothed back in a tight bun: our amah, Ah Lien. We expatriate babies with working mothers often spent a great deal of time with our amahs, and in fact it was Ah Lien I took as my linguistic model as I made my first attempts at human speech: a Hainanese baby language that was totally impenetrable to my astounded parents. Eager to communicate with their toddler and sorrowful that they could not do so, they engaged the services of a tutor in Hainanese to give them lessons in that island dialect. But their well-meaning efforts were all in vain. When, full of hope, they tried out their newly learned phrases on me, I would look at them as if they had gone insane. People with European faces did not speak my language. *Everybody* knew that! So I looked at my despairing progenitors with puzzlement and decided I would get back to them later.

I adored Ah Lien, and she was inordinately proud of me, carrying me around the neighborhood to visit her cronies and to show off my little party tricks. I was taught a series of Chinese nursery rhymes, which I would perform with great aplomb, amid much clapping and cheering in the servants' quarters of different houses. My parents, meanwhile, were teaching me all the games and stories that British children learn, including 'Round and Round the Garden' and 'Incy Wincy Spider'. But although I sang the little English songs to please my parents, the sheer hours put in by Ah Lien and the rest of the Hainanese contingent won out over my working parents, who only got to play with me in the evenings. I became a Hainanese-speaking child. Despite all the musical reinforcement from my faithful Hainanese fans, however, the very earliest childhood ditty that has stayed with me today reveals after all the triumph of my mother's voice, for it consists of fragments of a Welsh counting song she taught me, 'Cyfri'r Geifr'.

The author aged one with her amah, Ah Lien, learning Hainanese.

It wasn't until I was three and the family returned to Britain for my father's initial sabbatical that, separated from my nurse, I stopped speaking Hainanese. This first prolonged stay in an English-speaking world expunged any remembrance of that dialect from my toddler's mind. As I was now surrounded exclusively by European faces, I naturally became a European speaker. Nevertheless, the linguistic transition was by no means a smooth one. When my father left for Singapore ahead of us, I fell into a lengthy mutism, refusing to speak in either Hainanese or English. I was taken by my distraught mother to a pediatrician, whose learned diagnosis was that the only thing the matter with her eerily silenced mite was that she was missing her daddy. My mother was assured that I would chirp up again before long and that she was not to worry. The doctor was proven right, for, after my mother and I returned to Singapore, I was a speaking person again – a monolingual, English-speaking person.

One day my father took me to the cool, dark GH Café in Collyer Quay – a special treat after routine visits to the doctor. The café was mysterious, a spacious cavern of air-conditioned luxury. Tea trolleys decked out in white linen were being stealthily rolled from table to table. As my father, attempting to teach me to suck orange crush through a straw, enjoined me to 'whistle inwards', a white-coated Chinese waiter came over to our table. He bent over toward me so that he would be level with my contorted, bubble-blowing face. Then, smiling enticingly all the while, he uttered a string of sounds. He was answered with the makings of a tantrum brought on by speech I could not understand. My toddler fists shook in bewildered pre-school mode as thwarted reason geared up for the big outburst, perhaps the one I should have staged when first dropped among the unmitigated English. The waiter walked off, tray in hand, laughing very strangely. Everybody else at the table was laughing too. Unnerved, I abandoned my pop bottle.

'Daddy, why is that man laughing at me? What did he say?' I clamored, crestfallen before a world that had so rudely veered from my own point of reference. 'Why are you laughing? What did the man say?'

'Cakes,' reported my amused father, semantic theories clearly fighting for space in his head. 'He asked if you wanted cakes.'

I was furious. Naturally I wanted cakes! But why had the waiter asked me in Chinese? Couldn't he see I was a little *orang puteh*? And why hadn't my father stepped in to defend my interests? The explanation was even more frustrating than the incident itself. 'Don't you remember?' coaxed my father with a gentle smile. 'The waiters used to gather around to talk to you in Hainanese every time we came here.'

I was given my chocolate éclair anyway, but the incident has sat upon the surface of my mind ever since like an overgrown cat-scratch. I had no idea that I had ever spoken anything but English.

When I was four, my brother John was born. He was a beautiful, elfin child with blond hair that later kept its promise to turn red and eyes that had the slightest hint of an upward slant: 'Magyar eyes', my mother called them. There are no family stories about his acquisition of English, which I believe went smoothly, but, as he got older, he occasioned a thousand anecdotes about his scuttling about in monsoon drains after midget frogs or stealing off into the patch of jungle across the road from our house and coming home covered in leeches. When he was old enough, he went to a Roman Catholic kindergarten, but my mother withdrew him almost immediately to save him from sadistic nuns. We both played with neighbor children – a mixed lot of academic progeny from all sorts of countries and every kind of religion – and with the amahs' children. We were taken for walks to the Botanical

Gardens, where we flailed sticks in our puny hands, pretending to keep at bay the hordes of monkeys that would follow us about, begging for peanuts, which formed the highlight of the trip. We gulped down unknown berries, stared at flying foxes – the fruit bats that guzzled grape-like treats in the treetops – pasted our eyelids inside out with frangipani sap, pounced on wall lizards so they would drop their tails and wiggle off to safety. As I got older, our parents decided to have me educated at a local school and applied for a place at the prestigious Raffles Girls'. I was too late to be considered by that time, so, after due investigation of its academic program, I was sent to Anthony Road Girls' School instead. My brother continued to go to the British primary school we had both previously attended.

During the Anthony Road days, the happy merry-go-round of voices and dialects continued to revolve around us. Every weekday John and I formed part of a clamoring carload of children reciting their multiplication tables on the way to school. Some of us were bound for English-medium schools, others (our amah's children) to an establishment where everything was taught in Mandarin. As we bowled along the steamy road to formal education, we would all – regardless of school, grade or language – take up the chant 'One seven seven, two sevens fourteen, three sevens twenty-one', or whatever the multiplication table happened to be for that particular morning. Our amah's children knew all the tables by heart in English, whether or not they could say anything else. In the afternoons after school, John and I would watch our Chinese playmates do their sums with the aid of an abacus, which we never figured out, and would learn jolly little Mandarin songs with actions, all about growing up tall and strong by dint of exercise. One of these I can still sing today, at least comprehensibly.

Clare Colton was my very best friend in Singapore. She was a dark-haired English girl to whose parents I did not have to write thank-you notes after each weekend I spent at their huge, wooden house set on stilts within its own generous grounds. Looking back to those days, I realize that, had she and I continued to be friends, I may not have conceived the visceral fear and loathing of off-campus compatriots that was later to mark my view of myself so deeply. Be that as it may, her early death was a tragedy for us all.

Mr Colton was connected in some way to the administration of the island, and they were, my mother said, very serious people, although, as my father later reminisced, 'they used to keep Stilton cheese in port – an awful waste of Stilton!' I seem to remember that they had a cat rather than dogs, though I am not sure, and threw intuitively perfect birthday parties for Clare, notably one attended by a bearded, turbaned Sikh conjuror who made Mrs Colton's wedding ring – which she had reluctantly removed from her finger – turn up in a navel orange.

Having been an only child until the age of ten, Clare was used to talking to adults and was extremely articulate for her age. She also possessed an unselfconscious sophistication that sometimes made me feel very unformed. At nine years of age, when I was still blushing at the sight of pictorial nakedness, Clare was already sketching elegant nudes on a large grainy artist's pad and she sang a beautiful soprano with eerily adult voice control merely from following the famous divas on her parents' collection of operatic LPs. She wrote breathtakingly dramatic plays, which involved running swords through yowling dragons behind bushes and having the audience pay to get out rather than to get in. One day we snuck off a to get a couple of bottles of Coke, which in those days we still called Coca-Cola, from the Coltons' icebox, which was kept separate from their kitchen fridge and was used exclusively for soft drinks. We opened the creaky old door and were amazed to see that a very fat python had fallen asleep in a mountain of coils at the far end. We shut the door and ran off excitedly to report the news to Mr Colton.

'Mr Colton, there's a python in the icebox!' I reported breathlessly.

'Now that's surely not the case, is it, Carys?' asked Clare's father even-handedly.

'It's true, Daddy!' Clare assured him. 'We saw it just this minute! It is not a fabrication of our fevered young minds!'

Mr Colton was not a man accustomed to childish pranks. He looked at us uncomfortably. His daughter, however, convinced him that he should investigate and, after discreetly verifying our claims, he began to organize matters. The first step was to send us off to the movies in the care of the syce, a decision that seemed unfair. He then telephoned the fire brigade, and what that brave band actually did it was never our privilege to behold.

Clare's little sister Juliet was born, as I remember, on my birthday, January 10th, another occasion on which we were smuggled off quietly to the cinema. I do not know how this sudden change in the structure of her family affected Clare, for soon afterwards my family left for Kuala Lumpur and we lost touch with the Coltons.

A very strange thing happened a few years later. I used to spend half an hour or so at dusk every day in my parents' bedroom, chatting with my mother as she got ready for her night in town working on whichever play happened to be in rehearsal. These used to be happy, private moments, indeed the only ones when I could be sure of having my mother to myself, and the room was alive with my mother's special aura. On this particular occasion, I was taken aback as I entered the room, for it seemed to be saturated with Clare: it was as if her essence, or the aroma of her personality, were filling the room. I suddenly became aware that I missed her very much and needed to get in touch with her again. When I asked my mother if she could give me the Coltons' address in Singapore, she put me off vaguely with something about it being pointless as Clare had gone off to boarding school in England. Disappointed, I let the matter rest. A few days later, having more or less forgotten about the incident, I sensed the same Clare-like atmosphere in my mother's room, only this time with greater intensity. I pleaded with my mother, 'Can't you write to Clare's father and ask him for her address? I simply must contact her again!' Within a second I was shocked to see my mother's face crumple up in tears. 'How did you know?' she asked, clearly devastated. 'Clare died in England the very same day you asked about her. We tried to hide the notice in the papers from you... since you hadn't mentioned her for years, we thought there was no point in saddening you with the news.'

It turned out that Clare had suffered a fatal accident on her first day at boarding school. She had fallen and struck her head on an iron bedpost. Whenever I think of her now, I remember that final visit to be with me and let me know what I might never have otherwise discovered. I imagine her always as a current friend, maturing at the same age as myself and yet still my girlhood companion. It was the loss of someone quite irreplaceable.

Clare had begun to recede from my life just as I was becoming Malayanized: her leaving Singapore to become an English boarding-school girl occurred just a couple of years after I first threw myself wholeheartedly into the life of St Mary's Girls' School in Kuala Lumpur. This establishment had begun as a missionary endeavor, connected in some way to St Mary's Church downtown, and had later received government aid. It cost just a few dollars per month to attend (or was it per term?), and we had to buy our own books. The medium of instruction was English, and all students took obligatory classes in Malay. Two versions of this language were taught at St Mary's and many other government-aided schools in Malaysia: Malay proper, taught in special classes to ethnic Malay students, and what was then called *Bahasa Kebangsa'an* or 'National Language'. This latter was a less complex, more democratic tongue, intended as a lingua franca for all Malaysians. Apart from this, students of Chinese and Tamil backgrounds also took classes in either Mandarin or Tamil. This meant that many of my friends were reasonably fluent in three languages by the time they were sixteen or so, as they would also speak their native tongue at home: Gujarati perhaps, or Cantonese.

At the time I was at St Mary's, there were about forty-five girls in each class. About thirty would be Chinese, about ten Indian, and there would be a handful of Malays. There were also schools teaching exclusively in Malay, Tamil or Mandarin, attended primarily by students from more traditional or anti-colonialist families who preferred to have their children educated solely within their own culture, but many people considered that it would be of greater educational and social advantage to send their children to an English-medium school. I believe I was the first European pupil to attend St Mary's, though a few more were to turn up later as news got around about my presence there. In any case, all this did was add to the diversity that already reigned. The school tuck shop was a globetrotting gourmet's delight, a culinary reflection of the tastes of its patrons. One could buy steaming bowls of *mee hoon* and piquant *laksa* soup, *nasi goreng* or fried rice, spicy little Indian savories, bright red in color and served in banana leaves, sweet dumplings with meat inside, shrimp *kropok*, curry puffs (*samosas*), the entire range of salty Chinese treats in little packets – now, to my joy, easily obtainable in Chinese supermarkets worldwide – as well as sweet, gaudily colored 'European-style' cakes, imported chocolate bars, and hard candy of all kinds. My favorite snack was *sutong*, dried and flattened squid, which one nibbled from a square of white newsprint, savoring its delicious saltiness. As well as food, I got into sports, debating societies, the school yearbook, I made friends – loads of friends – and, above all, I began to learn Malay.

It seemed to me there was no language more limpid than Malay. It unsheathed no bristling consonant clusters, rasped up no gutturals, its vowels were pure and reliable – only six, as I remember, as opposed to the twenty odd that exist in English – and it was enunciated amid a series of optimistic glottal stops. The author of a well-known Malay textbook described it at the time as 'a flexible, eel-like language' in which emphasis is achieved not by urgency of tone, but through a subtle use of word order combined with gentle, but meaningfully presented intonation. I was mesmerized by its possibilities.

Once the grammatical idiosyncrasies of this agglutinating language had been sorted out, we were taught mysterious, poetic items called 'idioms'. I learned that it was considered crass to speak directly about unpleasant or inconvenient things, so one had to select the right idiom to describe a less than diplomatic situation with the appropriate delicacy. (Later in life I came across a fine passage featuring this elliptical mode of speech in Anthony Burgess' *Enemy In the Blanket*, which forms part of his riveting *Malayan Trilogy*. An 'enemy in the blanket' is a common Malay euphemism for what English describes as a snake in the grass, and the novel contains a cryptic, page-long, literal English translation of a rather nasty piece of village gossip expressed entirely in beautiful euphemisms.) Meanwhile, Malay had opened for me a world of multi-layered questions about language and reality.

Our teachers often addressed us as if trained by Enid Blyton, 'Now, girls, what does *kaki ayam* mean?'

Naturally *kaki ayam* – literally 'chicken-footed' – meant 'poor'. Why? Because the very poor can't afford shoes. And chickens don't wear shoes, do they?

Chicken-footed. Many years later, as an undergraduate on a year's study in Seville, I was taken aback to note that a common derogatory term in Spanish for someone poor and/or shiftless was *muerto de hambre*: 'starving to death', 'unable to keep body and soul together'. I remember my shock at the cruel engine that drove their scorn for the indigent. The favored expression for such a person in US English, however, mirrors a nation's attitudes just as faithfully: 'loser', one unable to win in the competition for a good life. So, to my thirteen-year-old mind, the relative gentleness of *kaki ayam* and its association of the poor with happy farmyard hens served as proof that the Malays were the nicest people in the world.

Today, decades later, I hear that *kaki ayam* (chicken-footed) does indeed mean 'poor' as I was taught, but for a scathing reason. It is a commonplace in Southeast Asia that people whose feet have not been restricted by shoes tend to have splayed toes, a condition that will be a sure giveaway for the rest of their lives. The poor are called chicken-footed because their spread-out toes resemble chickens' feet. So much for elegance! From the same person, I also discovered that the Indian greeting *namaste*, pronounced with the palms of the hands reverently placed together, means something along the lines of 'I see God in you'. This would have been enough, had I known it, to send me into rhapsodies over the beauty of Indian culture, except that I had already seen the caste system in action. But, in true textbook fashion, I was building a world in accordance with my dreams.

I received practical lessons in Malay euphemistic speech

every day from my friend Shahaneem, a quiet, humorous girl with huge brown eyes with whom I spent every lunch break for some years before we were split up into different classes. As one of the more academically promising girls in our year, she would normally have stayed in the top stream, but, as the only Malay student in our class and therefore the only one obliged to take *Bahasa Melayu* as well as Islamic Studies, she caused a scheduling nightmare and ended up being placed in another, more bureaucratically convenient class. We had been all but inseparable until that point.

One day, when the bell rang for the end of recess and it was time to get smartened up again for class – anything less was unthinkable then – I asked Shahaneem if I ought to comb my hair. Shahaneem blushed slightly. 'Well,' she said, and what followed was truly Versaillesque: 'It could possibly be thought that your hair would benefit from a certain amount of attention.' I understood her right away. She meant 'Do your hair, girlfriend, it looks like a bird's nest!'

Shortly before this memoir was due to go into print, I was saddened to hear of Shahaneem's passing. I would like to believe that the kindness, modesty and intellect she had always shown as a schoolgirl were known to all during her distinguished career as director of a famous national library and the author of a series of children's books in Malay, some of which have been translated into English.

What my highly selective memory now recalls of her speech is that it echoed 100% the old adage so often repeated to American girls: 'If you can't say anything nice, don't say anything at all.' Then again, Shahaneem's native language was totally set up for this kind of thinking. There is a particular prefix (*ter-*) that may be applied to any verb to imply that whatever action described by that verb was carried out unintentionally. The judicious use of *ter-* divests you of all responsibility, paints you as the passive party, keeps the butter from melting in your mouth and in many ways is reminiscent of the 'no-fault *se*' in Spanish. One day some Malay classmates told me that they had noticed (*ternampak*) my slip showing below the hemline of my school uniform, i.e. that they were aware of 'snow down south' – but only in spite of themselves, not because they were looking! Since the implications for diplomacy were infinite in Malay, it seemed to me, why should anyone choose to be direct about anything at all?

Among all this amiability and finesse, the Malay obscenities I would sometimes encounter on bathroom walls were like an incursion from another universe. (Actually, I only ever saw the same word over and over again and didn't have a clear idea about what it referred to, such was our ignorance.) But instead of seeing this graffiti as hard evidence of extant realities in Malay, I rejected the thought that anything rude or violent could ever be expressed in that language. I created a golden halo around the language and its speakers and gathered into my consciousness only those elements that would adorn me in the eyes of the Self, who was nourished – poor, starving thing – on the daily expressions of Others.

It wasn't that I had been sheltered from the realities of Malay life, as Gautama Buddha in his youth was kept from the painful aspects of existence, shown only young, healthy people, never being informed of deaths. I'd heard about the Maria Hertogh riots in the early fifties and I'd certainly witnessed rare but unedifying classroom catfights, one of which involved two fourteen-year-old classmates at Anthony Road, both apparently in love with the young Malay instructor who taught the class. As the hair flew and the nails scratched among screeched insults, the man had been totally unable to take charge of the situation and had kept his head buried helplessly between his crossed arms, his defeated body slumped like a dead weight on the desk before him. There was also the fact that some native Malay speakers were very occasionally subject to falling into *latah* (a minor variation of Tourette's syndrome), not to mention blood-seeking amok states. And I knew a few Malay people that I didn't much like. But these ordinary realities melted away before the charm of the structure and vocabulary of the Malay language, a glittering, delicately-nuanced palette with which I daubed the silhouettes in the coloring book of my early romance with language.

Optimistic young girls tend to be the object of the best of human generosity as well as of the worst of human depredations. I must have been a particularly favored girl, an altruistic adolescent in a nation whose search for a grip on its future identity paralleled my own. In any case, the siren song of the Malay language sounded notes that I was unable to resist. That syntax of graceful physicality, a fingerprint of quiet truth that I longed to press into the gaucheness of my all-too-British demeanor, gave me hope for the woman I aspired to become.

I began to be embarrassed for the English language, associated in my mind with red, sweaty faces, loud voices, overtly needy and inappropriately expressed sexuality. Well-bred Malays avoided grimacing, eschewed the comical body language employed in convivial contexts that I thought coarsened the English social scene. They didn't puff and spit their way through their language, as it seemed to me that the English did, but were very decently self-contained, safe from unseemly overspill, either physical or emotional.

I began to hear spoken English through what I imagined to be Malaysian ears and would have ripped out my tongue. Instead, my English pronunciation became prim, pruned and sanitized. When with my friends, I lapsed naturally into the melting-pot

Malaysian English accent, barely distinguishing between 'p's and 'b's, inserting a *lah* everywhere for emphasis:

'Ahmad would be just right for you, *lah*!'

'No, *lah*, too skinny, *lah*!'

At home, I must have sounded like a character in a satirical play. I remember discussions with my mother, who tried to convince me that I sounded like an idiot saying 'sand-wiches', emphasizing the 'd', because this was not, regardless of its spelling, the correct way to pronounce the word. My mother pronounced it 'sanwiches' with a slight hint of a 'g' – still a far cry from the loathsome 'samwiches'. What was all this laxness? Where was linguistic propriety? In vain, my father told me some rigmarole about George Bernard Shaw and his point about the need for a new spelling of the anarchical English language, which might as well write 'fish' as 'ghoti' (with 'gh' pronounced as in 'cough', 'o' as in 'women' and 'ti' as in 'nation'), and that I should put a sock in my new mode of pronouncing 'forehead' literally and stick to the correct family version of 'forred'. It was all much too Neanderthal for my blood. I wanted no clumping in my mouth, no spittle.

It was not until I began to study phonetics at York University that I learned about the moving parts of the mouth and throat and how vowels and consonants edged themselves this way and that in accordance with different factors, but always in a tendency toward greater ease of pronunciation. I also learned the mind-blowing concept that a written grammar should be taken as *descriptive* of the language of its educated native speakers, not *prescriptive* of it, unless one was French and abided by the strictures of the Academie.

Where had I been shamed by the lolling beer belly of English as she is spoke? Certainly not at home. My mother's use of English was blithe, earthy and emphatic. She spoke in a happy mixture of high-register terminology and the best of British slang, along the lines of: 'What's that truculent little bugger up to now?' But her Welsh emphasis sometimes tinged my ears with fire as she quickened the colors of my carefully leached vocabulary. My father's speech was precise, analytical: a reasonable, discreet language I could comfortably confess to owning. Nevertheless, my mother's instinctual use of language and her conviction that you could express anything at all under God's bright sun if only you tried hard enough – and weren't too fussy about linguistic perfection – made her an outstanding communicator on the practical level. In possession of approximately three words of pidgin Malay and none of any dialect of Chinese except Hainanese, she would go to the live-chicken stall in the Singapore market, pick out a chicken and, by means of a variety of pantomimed gestures, be able to ask the Cantonese stall owner to kill that particular chicken and have it plucked and cleaned while she got the rest of her shopping done. (Negotiating a price was a piece of cake.) My father, on the other hand, would never say anything at all in a foreign language unless he could manage to say it in a manner that would amount to a faithful representation of the layered implications of his everyday English speech: hard to do, but he did bring it off in Mandarin on one or two memorable, bombshell-like occasions after due and intensive practice in his study. To steal a quote from Shakespeare, as far as linguistics was concerned, both my parents to themselves were entirely true and therefore could not be false to any man. However, in English, my mother was by far the better schmoozer, though my father was an ace at long-drawn-out, late-night confabulations with cronies.

 Conversations with my parents were eye-openers, especially as regards the doings of the expatriates that lived around us in campus housing. Mr Musgrove could sometimes be seen in his yard of an evening intently covering clean dishes with dirt so that his amah 'would have something to do for her salary' on quiet days. Miss Smith, a rather mature au pair and ostensible ballet dancer, had had to appeal to the High Commission of her native New Zealand to pay her passage home, thanks to the depredations of the academic whose overstretched wife, Melinda, had hired her to take care of the kids. This same botanist had passed off his married graduate student as his spouse at a conference abroad and was only caught when their hosts wrote to his department chair, saying how pleased they were that Professor Benton had been able to bring along his delightful wife, Indira. I was also coached by my mother – who would gleefully act them out – in the juicier elements of every British accent that seeped into our circle and in every humorous idiosyncrasy of caste and community that came to light. I have loved speech modes ever since – all types and in all languages, foreign, regional, class, educational, faux – absolutely all and, although I was not too brilliant a mimic, I did become quite handy at identifying them. All this seemed natural and intrinsic to listening to what you were being told, and I was as much shocked later on in life by Americans who believed that the Beatles spoke with Cockney accents as by some of the local expatriates who couldn't distinguish a Malay from a Chinese from a Sikh.

My aversion to the British must have stemmed from my fear of being taken for one of them. I knew very few British people my own age, and the ones I had seen were army children: not the ones sent home to boarding school, but those who lived out their fathers' tours in a failed simulacrum of home and attended their own school, where paternal military rank ruled supreme and everyone knew everybody else's father's salary to the cent. The parents of these children were very different from mine, who were university- and theater-circle types. I had never noticed any army people in our living room, where, it seemed to me, every human species in the known universe availed itself of my parents' hospitality and my mother's sympathetic ear. Those very foreign Others on the army school bus that came by for my brother were at the same time a threat and my heart's desire. I longed for the oblivious insouciance of their lives and was terrified that the world would shovel me onto the bus with them.

These thoughts, however, would become irrelevant once I arrived at school, where life was far too entertaining to be concerned with such matters. We learned the history and geography of Asia as well as Arithmetic, English, National Language, Physical Training, Hygiene and Singing. Singing class was based on folk songs from around the world sung out of old Edwardian songbooks printed long before the rule of Eton-cropped Miss Carpenter, the first headmistress I recall after Mrs Pestana of Anthony Road Girls' School in Singapore. This accounts for my knowledge to this day of a fine array of fatuous, pan-European folk songs about girls with nut-brown hair, people who gather violets in the dew and lusty young men who love their lederhosen. I can also shriek the descant of 'The Happy Wanderer', which somehow always made its way into the program at Parents' Night, to my mother's abiding horror. All I remember from Hygiene was the importance of getting rid of all standing water to eliminate chances of malaria, that cross-ventilation was a necessity in every room and that we should put on clean clothes every day. Ah, and that babies should not be given condensed milk because the chubbiness it gave them was all from sugar, not from good health. I dimly remember classes about Genghis Khan, Kemal Atatürk, Shah Jahan and the Mughal emperors, as well as a few of the Chinese luminaries.

We also had a great deal of English Literature, always taught very carefully and enjoyably, if somewhat irrelevantly. A well-meaning, beleaguered substitute English teacher who was not as smart as our usual instructors (and who, like them, was not a native speaker) once incorrectly edited a composition I'd written, which caused much repressed fury on my part. Infused with a firm and very Asian respect for teachers, I was much too polite to point out her errors to her, preferring to suffer in silence since she was only taking two classes with us. In general, though, life was good and our teachers were excellent.

There were so many children in need of education, and so few schools to accommodate them, that some schools began to work in two shifts. If I remember correctly, the morning shift would begin at seven thirty with assembly and end at about one thirty, and the afternoon session would start shortly thereafter, ending at around seven thirty in the evening. To make things equitable, different years switched sessions every term. Most of us disliked the afternoon shift, as it often threw us out of kilter with friends from other, single-shift schools. It also meant that contact with our peers would end as school let out, something I found particularly trying. Normally, on days when I didn't have training for the hundred-meters dash that was my specialty, I would get out of school looking forward to the Foch Avenue bus-stop experience, take the bus home, shower, eat, dispatch any homework and then conduct my social life at friends' houses, returning to Number 2, Road 12/5, at seven o'clock on the dot. Then it would be time to socialize with the home front: my mother as she got ready for her evening, my father as he glided up and down, preparing his lectures, any odd habitués of the house lounging, drink in hand, on my parents' furniture and getting in some good conversation. I usually ignored my little brother, who was often in bed anyhow at that time, though revelations made in later years about his afternoon social activities in the environs of Petaling Jaya made me realize I had missed a lot of boy-stuff derring-do, such as when he and Johnny Wong once frightened some machine-gun-toting security guards by creeping up behind them and shouting 'boo!' Soon after saying hello to the visitors, it would be time to get ready for bed, which meant writing my diary (in a fat, red hardcover renewed every Christmas as a present from my mother) and doing my devotions (from my maroon, leather-bound Bible and a printed booklet with designated daily prayers suitable to a Christian person of my age) before falling asleep.

For a while, I employed a trick I had developed to avoid dreaming of unpleasant subjects. I would lie half asleep in bed, lining up in my mind's eye any and all disagreeable people or concepts in front of a guillotine. The line would consist of personalities and ideas as varied as Frankenstein, Mrs Osman, the science teacher, the amorous but spotty Raymond Chang from up the road, a lump representing a current cholera scare, another lump to stand for an embarrassing event that had occurred at school and so on. When I had accounted for absolutely everything I could possibly think of that I did *not* want to see in my dreams, I would carefully add three or four extra lumps, representing 'Things I Had Not Thought Of'. These were to cover both those items I knew and had simply forgotten to include and those I still didn't know about and so could not add to the list. Once this was done, I callously sent the assembled company through the guillotine. This was done in a somewhat hazy, symbolic fashion, so those that were lumps and had no heads could be decapitated just as thoroughly as the human bogies. The method never failed, and I recommend it to anyone, with the caveat that it doesn't work unless you put in enough headless lumps.

One of the headless lumps was failure at school. It was vastly clear to all of us that, if we were not properly educated and had the certificates to prove it, we would end up as third-world beggars and bring shame to our country. We were proud of our schoolmates who did well academically, whether or not we had any clue about the subjects they were studying. Girls who did well at sports were also admired, but only in a transient sort of way.

One Monday, a sign was put up in a corridor: 'SILENCE PLEASE – LATIN EXAM IN PROGRESS'. Latin! How exotic that sounded, and how *hard*! We were told that one of the senior girls was planning to apply to medical school in England and had been coached specially for this prerequisite. Public exams were sacred to us. We dropped all non-academic activities as a matter of course a month or so before we had to sit for the Lower Certificate of Education and other such trials. Some girls, whose parents had told them they would be disowned if they did not do well, wept at their results. Our hope was to go on to the Sixth Form at the Victoria Institution and from there take our university entrance exams two years later. The choice place for study was Oxford or Cambridge; failing that (and most mortals did fail that), the very prestigious University of Malaya. In third but still prideful place would be any British university, and then, trailing far behind, came the vast ignominy of Australia.

It was only the Muslim girls at school who were prohibited by law from attending the religious rites of other groups: they were not even allowed to be present at our school's daily assembly, which included short prayers and a hymn. Chinese girls of various religions attended, as did the Hindus, and any school news was passed on to the Muslim girls later. None of this difference in our faiths mattered to us at all, except as a means of helping us understand each other's customs. As far as we were concerned, the more religions there were among us, the merrier things would be.

It must have been so easy to manipulate our youthful altruism, and the massed dances in which we were sometimes required to participate combined our pride in our differences with our desire to belong together, providing a perfect propaganda tool for certain political groups. What wonderful youth, that of Malaysia! Regardless of hues and creeds, we worked together in loving harmony to build our emerging nation. With hundreds of other girls from all over the state of Selangor, I danced at Merdeka Stadium for the Independence Day celebrations. We were all dressed in sleek batik sarongs with close-fitting, hip-length, yellow or orange *kebayas*, craftily coordinated among each group of dancers for a particular choreographical effect, and we sinuously waved lace shawls in coordinating colors. There had been a group from every school – Mandarin-, Malay- or Tamil-medium as well as English-medium establishments like St Mary's – and every group had been trained separately from the others, joining together only for the massive dress rehearsal a day or so before the great event. As we began to dance, it was clear that each ethnic group was translating the gestures of the piece into its own particular aesthetic. The dance was a kind of whimsical modern ballet based loosely on Malay folk patterns, and its movements were intended to represent the rising of the sun over the paddy fields, the graceful awakening of the peasant woman, the dibbling of the ground for the sowing of seeds, the harvesting of the crop, the threshing of the grain and, at the end, the joy of a job well done in communion with nature.

We wide-eyed young Malaysian dancers, though, felt that the choreography was embarrassingly vapid and had only agreed to take part because we were let off classes to do so and had heard that our male counterparts would be doing some massed gymnastics displays. Although we never had a chance to watch our performance – videos had not yet been invented and hardly anybody had television – the coordination of our movements must have been impressive from the stands, for at several points the stadium broke out in applause and some of the boys later told us that our dance had been beautiful.

National Language Day was, however, quite another thing. Contingents from all the schools marched through town to Merdeka Stadium, holding placards exhorting people to 'Speak Malay!', 'Speak the National Language!' This was a great social event, much less regimented than the floaty dance had been. As usual, I had been among those inveigled into taking part, since my reddish head among all the black-haired ones would help to emphasize the concept of interracial brotherhood. We marched along in an endless, straggling file, youths of all the ethnicities of the land, the bright hope of the country's future, chattering together happily and positively in good Malaysian English!

I have no idea whether the march had been presented in the press as voluntary or our teachers had been ordered to rustle us up, but we really believed in it. The Malays were the *bumi putera* – princes of the land – who had arrived in the Malay Peninsula before the Chinese and Indian emigrants and belonged to the same ethnic group as the ruling aristocracy. It was their language that had been chosen as the National Language, the language of all Malaysians. Nobody – at least not in my youthful circle – questioned the sociopolitical implications of choosing one language above another. Speakers all of the National Language, we never saw how the decision would affect the rest of the land, the pivotal role its use would play in the job market and centers of power, regardless of individual ability. Certain financial and other advantages were being given to urban Malays – those outside of the main cities were mostly employed in agriculture – in order to even out the economic balance between the main ethnic groups in the country. The real racial tension exploded in the bloody riots of 1969, three years after I left Malaysia. The quota system left by the British had finally caused the country to burst at the seams, causing the Constitution and Parliament to be suspended for three years of horror that many Malaysians can still not bring themselves to mention. But, for many of us, in 1961, the full implication of 'job' was still too far away and, for me in particular, the public defense of my beloved Malay as the National Language made me coequal with my many Chinese and Indian friends and encouraged my belief that we had a destiny together in that emerging country.

However, despite our diversity (or perhaps because of it), people would sometimes wander into trouble, as once happened with my first boyfriend's sister, Cecilia. Together with their brother, Leslie, they were a true Malaysian mix. Their father's family was Sri Lankan; their mother was Portuguese-Eurasian on her Indian father's side and Malay on that of her mother, who was probably descended from the famously matriarchal Minangkabau community of Negeri Sembilan. So perhaps it was not all that surprising that Ceci was interrupted by a police officer one Ramadan morning as she innocently munched on a curry puff from a street-side hawker.

'Aren't you ashamed?' asked the police officer fiercely.

'No, why?' responded Ceci with her usual curiosity, wiping her mouth with a wax-paper napkin. The man, beet red, gave it another try.

'Aren't you ashamed?' he repeated, determined not to elaborate. Ceci realized in a flash what had happened. The man thought she was Malay, and therefore Muslim, breaking the religious fast in public. Only the sick, the pregnant, those traveling and menstruating women were exempt. The police officer thought that Ceci was being rather too free in advertising a certain physiological state. Ceci, however, wasn't about to be shamed.

'But I'm a Christian!' she retorted loudly, settling her glasses more firmly on her defiant-looking nose. 'I can eat when I like!' The policeman scuttled off, even redder than before.

A dear friend of mine, a Sikh girl called Charan Kaur who lived a few blocks away from us in Petaling Jaya, was a walking mishmash of religious influences. Every year, during a Taoist festival in which gastronomic delicacies were set outside houses for the enjoyment of visiting ancestral spirits, sometimes entire streets would be lined with offerings of lacquered duck, piles of pretty mandarin oranges, sweet cakes, 'hundred-year-old eggs' and anything else that might tempt the appetite of Chinese ancestors. One simply passed on by, avoiding undue interest, and certainly never even dreamed of helping oneself to the food. Charan's kid sister, Ranjit, was walking home from their convent school one day, as usual absolutely famished. Coming upon a mouth-watering display outside one of the neighbors' houses and thinking that the food must have been put out to join the garbage, she grabbed hold of a bunch of *pisang emas* (tiny, plump golden bananas), broke a couple off and began to peel the first one. By the time she got to her front gate, she was swallowing down the last bite, the telltale banana skins dangling from her hand. As she realized what had happened, Charan started to scream.

'What the hell do you think you're doing?' she howled, slamming the gate behind them and herding her sister across the yard and into their bungalow. 'Where did you get those bananas?'

'I just stole a couple from somebody's trash!' hiccupped Ranjit. 'They'll never notice!'

This didn't mollify Charan at all. She stopped thumping Ranjit's skinny little back and started to shake.

'You fool,' she wept, hiding her face in her hands. 'You're not just a thief. Those bananas were meant for the spirits! Now they'll come and get you in the night! They'll come and snatch your nose off, like you snatched their bananas! Oh, my God! *Pisang emas* too!'

'What shall I do? What shall I do?' wailed Ranjit, never overly resourceful at the best of times. She covered her face with twitching hands. The two sisters sniffled loudly in unison for a minute. All of a sudden Charan jumped up in a clatter, scattering the low stool she had been sitting on. She was beaming.

'I know!' she shouted. 'Say ten Hail Marys! That'll fix it!'

Much as we laughed at all the ingredients in Charan's confused religious stew, in fact they had a firm underpinning in the traditional faith of her family, which was Sikhism, an Islam-influenced offshoot of Hinduism that accepts all religious manifestations as part and parcel of a greater, all-encompassing force. She had been merely playing off different aspects of the same thing against each other, as a child plays off one parent against the other.

The lessons most emblazoned on my mind were, of course – where in the world are they not? – the ones picked up in classroom psychology and schoolyard politics. In the case of St Mary's, the experiences were deeply layered, as we had racial, religious and linguistic considerations to add to the manifold foibles of the unfolding human personality. We were certainly not ignorant as far as religions went, as we had official days off for all the main Christian religious holidays of the nation. Apart from Christmas, Easter and Whitsun, we were also off for Ascension Day: we were, after all, an Anglican school. The Muslim holy days included the great feast of the end of

Ramadan – the date of so many memorable get-togethers – and the Prophet's birthday. We were also free on Thaipusam and on Diwali, the festival of lights, for Chinese New Year, the sultan's birthday and the king's birthday. We made the rounds of our friends' houses on their feast days and expected to be visited on ours, and the sampling of foods was always wide-ranging and voluminous. We took meticulous care to observe each other's cultural and religious customs. In fact, one of the reasons I joined the Anglican Church was to have a religion with rituals and beliefs as all my friends did.

The diaries of those years are a chronicle of two things: the Byzantine, sometimes heartbroken convolutions of the affairs of my heart and my impassioned compliance with what was clearly propaganda. All my triumphs in the school Malay debating team, all my appearances on youth-centered radio shows, the picture in the paper after my sugary role in the historical pageant as a seventeenth-century Dutch-girl colonist jumping puddles on the way to church, the graceful dance en masse in Merdeka Stadium, my vision of a shining, egalitarian Malaysia – all that sincerity was but one more ingredient flung into a slow-cooking pot by the policy makers of that emerging nation.

Nevertheless, my life at that time was supremely happy and lived intensely. I had a huge network of friends, and many more people, it seemed, wanted to meet me. From among a well-stocked little crowd of teenaged swains from the athletics meets, the church youth club, the brothers and cousins of my female friends from school and the Petaling Jaya neighborhood, my first boyfriend emerged. From the end of 1963 to well after we left in 1966, I was very much in love with the same delightful, talented, loyal young man, David, whose affection imprinted a necessary grace note on my subsequent essays in matters of the heart.

But I lived this life in a bravado of sincerity, aching to belong, determinedly ignoring the also sincere curiosity quotient or glamour factor at work among those who were not my closest friends. I clearly remember the young man who followed my father and me nearly all the way home on his scooter, smiling and waving, and the boys who would call to introduce themselves as friends of friends. At all times, though immensely flattered, my first reaction would be to assume Malaysianness, to make it clear that I was not exotic and was certainly not like Other European Girls. And I was happy believing my own propaganda.

By the time I was twelve or so, I had begun to write – usually rather mawkish poems – and I would copy these down, along with pieces by other authors I liked, into a lined, marbled notebook. I was also keeping a diary, a habit I maintained until we arrived in Jamaica in 1966 and have continued sporadically ever since. I never wrote in anything but English, although I was perfectly capable of doing so in Malay. Within the bounds of those neutral, dated pages, I could avail myself of the English I loved, spoken on my terms and yet endlessly generous. I was quite unable to gauge – nor would it ever have crossed my mind to do so – the level of my command of English or writing ability against that of other English speakers my age. Naturally I did well in English at school, I thought – I *was* English, or as near as dammit, and so I'd had a good, stiff leg up. I had no mirror in which to see my face.

Just as my Malaysian identity was beginning to coalesce again, it seemed that my father would have another sabbatical due and we would make the trip (first-class by BOAC, as I remember) to my grandmother's home in Swansea. It soon became too onerous for my father to tutor us during those three-month stays, so after a while we were sent to local schools: my brother to Swansea Grammar School (a secondary school for academically oriented boys) and I to Llwyn-y-Bryn Girls' School, a similar outfit for the opposite gender. I was placed in the languages stream, though I had no French or Latin, because my father had given me some lessons in elementary German so that I would be familiar with another European language. My best friend at that school was Olivia Pompa, who took French, Latin, German and Spanish and belonged to a group of Italian origin known as the 'ice-cream Welsh' because they had opened ice-cream parlors when they first emigrated to Britain. Olivia helped me navigate the very stern rules of that establishment and immersed me in soccer fandom on the occasional weekend, when with a group of classmates we would go and watch a certain gorgeous goalie defend Swansea's honor on all our behalves. I had often heard Welsh spoken in my grandmother's house by older family friends, and my mother could still speak a smattering, but the school introduced me to Welsh in a more formalized manner. We sang Welsh hymns regularly at daily assembly: that is, the other girls did, I merely stumbled along trying to figure out the pronunciation, which the Welsh are blithely convinced is 'completely phonetic'. (Yes, but in *what* phonetic system?) Nevertheless, I loved the hymns for the mystery of my past that they enshrined, full of heartfelt sentiment and a sense of awe at the beauties of creation. Poetry and song were revered at Llwyn-y-Bryn, and there was a yearly eisteddfod or musical competition in which girls from different school-wide 'houses' or teams participated. Like the Welsh National Eisteddfod, the proceedings were opened by an important figure (the head girl in our case) garbed in druidical robes designed by nineteenth-century Celtic Twilightists. The girl would half unsheathe a gigantic wooden sword and call out three times, '*A oes Heddwch?*' ('Is there peace?'). When the assembled company had thrice shouted back, '*Heddwch!*' ('Peace!'), the girl would put away her sword, and the competition proper would begin.

This daft pantomime would make me quiver with excitement and a sense of belonging. I felt very much a member of the Welsh community, although I'd had so little contact with Wales and hardly knew what such belonging meant. To this day I weep when I hear a good Welsh male voice choir, especially if they manage to work themselves up into *hwyl*, an ecstatic, lyrical musical state that is hard to describe but immediately apparent in the voice. Stories abounded about the lives of well-known Welsh harpists, piano players or singers, all of whom were revered. In fact, my first published article was about Telynores Tawe, the Harpist of Swansea, a title bestowed on her at an eisteddfod. She was a family friend, whom my mother and grandmother invariably addressed as Telynores ('Telly-nor-iss'), although they knew her real name. Her beautiful, old concert harp, standing near the fireplace in her tiny living room, imbued the whole house with a magical aura, despite the fact that its owner, when I met her, was a sweetly garrulous, birdlike old lady with bright eyes and a huge comic sense who would take happy swigs just before she fell asleep from a daily bottle of Guinness she hid behind her green bedroom curtains. Our visit was unforgettable in that it linked me more closely with the Welsh musical tradition in which my mother and grandmother had been raised: a mythical pool now enriched with a sea of overwhelming monsoon rain.

The influence of American popular culture was by this time taking hold of some of the urban population in West Malaysia. Young people listened to rock music, pop idols and country and western with equal fervor. I myself was a fan of Chet Atkins (I had only heard the one song – 'Your Cheatin' Heart' – but it was enough), Cliff Richard (how *could* I?) and Dave Brubeck (I thought 'Take Five' was the best thing I'd ever heard on the radio) and, when the Beatles appeared on the scene, I joined the global squabble over which was the cutest. I found the Rolling Stones distasteful and crude, likewise the gyrations of Elvis Presley, though I adored his voice in the slower songs. But young folk all around me were soon much more into rock and roll, and one Chinese girl in my class, a smart kid called Christine Lim, actually took a day off from school to go to Kuala Lumpur airport and scream along with several other hundred teenagers when Cliff Richard's plane touched down. This she did without ever having shown any signs of fandom or any form of rebellion against her own particular social or cultural situation: it was the modern thing to do, so she did it. We all thought she was nuts. Some of the Chinese, Malay and Indian boys would dress up like American rock idols and have their hair styled to match, but the general opinion was that, although this gave them an overtly sexy veneer, the more they tried to look like pop stars, the less likely they were to be good catches when the time came.

I found all this Americanization horrifying. I became very apprehensive to see that the very people in whom I sought sanctuary from my own shamefully uncontrolled race were actively going out of their way to lose their composure. Apart from this – and this was a big thorn in the side of my language-oriented psyche – I couldn't understand why it was necessary for British bands to sing in American accents, much less Malaysian groups. And why were people going crazy over songs and movies that described young people behaving in ways that generally seemed out of line for most Malaysians? It never quite dawned on me that most of the people I knew, by attending English-speaking schools, wearing western clothes and spending time (within certain limits) in mixed groups, were already highly westernized. If I had thought about it at all, I would probably have concluded this meant they were simply modern, more modern, for example, than the girls who went to Tamil- or Mandarin-medium schools. Everybody had guidelines evolved and adapted within their own social group and knew that these included the circumstances in which young men and women would finally, often irrevocably, pair off with each other. Some young people were actively breaking away from the more repressive rules – particularly some of the young Malays, who were all Muslims, and Indians, who had the caste system to deal with – behind their parents' backs, but they were doing this in their own ways, as Malaysians, not faux Americans. I must have thought that westernization was one thing, Americanism quite another – or was it that subconsciously I only approved of Europeanization? Whatever lay beneath my attitude, one thing was clear: Americans were English speakers, and so was I. I had to keep a safe distance. I had to show them I was intrinsically different from them, but the only mark of differentiation they were capable of understanding was that I was a standoffish Brit and they were hang-loose Americans. Being corralled into the one-size-fits-all British-girl category was a prospect I was still unable to face.

Just as I was searching in the language and psychology of other communities for elements that would help me find someone to be, so were my friends. But the influence of some American icons took a deep hold on all of us. James Dean was for years after his death a favorite spirit to be conjured up on the Ouija board, a ghost who would understand your anguished teenage soul no matter what country you came from. But one thing was a person's teenage soul and quite another his or her preparation for marriage, which, as some of my friends were very much aware, was likely to drop suddenly and irrevocably from above with no warning, like a curtain at the end of a middle-school skit. Charan Kaur, my dearest friend among our Petaling Jaya neighbors and the one who had saved her sister from the angry Chinese spirits, was a tall, gauche girl who scandalized her Sikh family and their circle by defying their religious custom of never taking a knife to one's hair. To make matters worse, Charan had got her hair cut in a jaunty pageboy to sing in a Talentime, which in her mother's eyes placed her in a moral category several steps beneath a kickline dancer. 'Who will marry you now?' her mother would nag, a note of shrill panic in her voice. 'Do you know what everybody thinks you are? You have disgraced your family!' But Charan was as oblivious of the need to put oneself on the marriage market as I was. We chose the role of teenagers, not brides. As such, we would talk about life, listen to the new records (Bobby Vee, Ricky Nelson), learn all the dances and go off to visit other friends to do the same all over again. And, although we refused to consider marriage as anything more than a dreamlike state too far in the future even to consider as pending, sentimental politics were very much to the fore in our conversations. But, for Charan, American-style teenhood would never dovetail into an American-style marriage, at least not as long as she remained in Kuala Lumpur. Last heard of, she was happily married to an Irishman in Melbourne, was the mother of two Aussie girls and was working as a biology teacher – a happy surprise to me after news of a wretched time in Kashmir, where she had been living on a houseboat and attending medical school, heartbrokenly and fearfully in love with someone she wasn't allowed to be in love with.

A different state of affairs obtained with another close friend from the neighborhood, the diminutive Sameera, a beautiful Malay girl about three years older than myself, who was my role model. She seemed to me to be the essence of wisdom and sophistication. She was friends and relations with a seemingly endless number of discreetly elegant, easy-going Malay guys with titles and affectionate, attentive manners. Sameera was coming up to the age when somebody in a situation to do something permanent about it might consider falling in love with her. (Serial dating was not something Malay girls seemed to do at that time, and any romantic overtures had therefore to be very carefully mapped out.) Although she enjoyed the attention of many male friends and entertained them with charming conversation and the latest records, I think she was waiting for a certain man to make his move. I never met him and I believe he was enough years older than she to have a serious job and probably even more serious prospects in government. She spoke about him if they had seen each other at some party or he had dropped by, but she never disclosed much more than her happiness at having seen him again. Toward the end of my years in Kuala Lumpur, she became less and less available to hang out, and I believe her ship was drawing nearer and nearer to the twinkling harbor lights we had all seen in the distance. I heard she became engaged just after we left Malaysia.

Many (though by no means all) of the young Malays attached to royal families tended to keep to themselves. The men belonged to the group from which the higher-level government administrators would often be appointed and, although they were polite and affable with everybody else, after a certain age they seemed only seriously interested in cultivating people of the same background. Sameera once took me along to one of their parties, where I had an impression people found me vaguely amusing but I was being politely offloaded from one nice young man to another. This somewhat older group was certainly less openly spirited than the people who frequented the parties I usually attended, and there was an almost imperceptible, trance-like vibe in the air, as where people are smoking reefer. The slow dances were done in total darkness – the lights were switched off to avoid the police having to notice that Muslim men and women were touching bodies – and then the lights came on again for the twist or the cha-cha-cha. I was unnerved to find myself dancing to a song that was later to remind me of the scandalously orgasmic gasps of Serge Gainsbourg's '*Je t'aime... moi non plus*' in pitch darkness with a man I had just met that very second, who was just being courteous to some kid dragged along by a friend. Everyone seemed very much, though very languidly, aware that at the party there existed some kind of future sexual opportunity. Sexuality was a given, it was merely, by tacit understanding, being smoothly invoked for more propitious circumstances. This was not a stage my friends had reached – or, if they had, their parties involved much more eclectic interests. I felt chastened, a little perplexed – wasn't all this supposed to be rather infra dig? But how could anything this smooth, worldly, rarefied group do possibly be infra dig? And all my other friends now looked like loud, gawky adolescents in comparison with my most recent dance partners. There were certainly no Elvis impersonators here! I was disquieted.

As a teenager at that time I was deeply in love, deeply aware of David's reactions, very easily flung into extremes of misery and joy by a simple word or look, a phone call that never came through, a contretemps in a schedule that might cause me to miss half an hour of his presence. I longed for his company. I longed for an unexpected opportunity for him to brush my hair or shoulder with his hand, a rare chance maybe to exchange a kiss. All this among the hectic activities of a bright young person's crammed academic and social life, the grist of a happy mill of other human beings, all intriguing to me, all as active as we were. For ours was a very public courtship, an embryonic affair that developed as we walked between engagements among the streets of Kuala Lumpur, participated together in church youth-club activities, danced the night away at parties. Some of our closest moments were spent chatting on the phone. Though I was aware of a growing desire for him, it was still unarticulated, unspecific, and I possessed no real pattern to indicate the direction of an acceptable next step.

Perhaps because my head was swirling with ideas about the million things that fascinated me, I lived in a world that was strangely asexual. We lacked the constant bombardment of packaged, commercialized allusions to sexuality that are so much a part of today's cityscape and media. The atmosphere in many ways reflected the girdled, pointy-bra'd, coy fifties, when nothing about sex was openly accepted in polite society, but everything revolved around it nonetheless, masquerading as a sort of manic cuteness. I witnessed nothing in my parents' vaguely bohemian environment to spark a single light that might indicate in practical terms this was all about something real that might someday happen to me, be a part of my life, an important part of who I was. Although their friends were having affairs all the time, affairs which they would confess to my mother, who would later sometimes tell me about certain aspects of them, whatever it was all seemed so blasé, so socialized.

The author with her dog Tommy (on the left) and Fifo at Petaling Jaya in 1965.

I had no elder sisters to observe as they passed through puberty into womanhood – and therefore no erotic vibrations to absorb – and the movies I saw were generally hectic portrayals of energetic American teenhood interspersed with kissing portrayed either as dreamy (with the good boyfriend) or verging on the violent (with the bad boy). My girl friends at the time were mostly still in the 'loves-me-loves-me-not' stage or else too blinded by the sweetness of newly declared love to think of taking too many steps beyond it. And the subject of fulfilled sexuality was totally taboo: we girls spoke only of undying love, never of sensuality. The sexually explicit metaphors of certain pop songs we were still happily interpreting in a spiritual sense, though apparently, it later turned out, most of our boyfriends were not. And, though I might well have been initiated into more detail by the lurid nightlife of Kuala Lumpur, this did not exist to me, busy as I was in my world of teen parties and 'boys'.

The author with her mother and brother at Kuala Lumpur Zoo in 1965.

Virginity was a part of my identity that was by no means a burden. I knew that one day I would be a grown-up and my current fledgling sexuality would take flight, though what that actually meant was still very much an unknown quantity. Before my relationship with David had coalesced into a reality, I had, like everyone else, gone through the hormonal turmoil of adolescence and a number of romantic skirmishes with different youngsters from the neighborhood, with none of whom I was allowed out by myself since I was considered too young at fifteen to be dating. The diary entries of my fourteenth year reveal an almost comically overwhelming emotional upheaval. But as soon as David and I had finally made our feelings known to each other – after almost a year of intensely enjoyable, very close friendship slashed through by agonizing doubt regarding the other's wish for anything further – I became more settled. It was as if the happiness we felt in each other had become anchored and focused. Love, in fact, had conquered all of that chaos. I began to live what was for me at least a blissful phase: desiring, desired, but not yet pressured by my body, my understanding or my partner to step into the exhilarating terrain of sexual exploration, much less to take the leap which, I somehow understood, would instantly encroach upon the idealized, independently formed sense of self that was always just beyond my grasp.

Of course, such deferment of this kind of knowledge, whether theoretical or in practice, was not to be the case for everybody. Some of my Indian friends had already been promised in marriage and would ultimately receive some form of instruction at home from their mothers. Other girls – though none known to me – had no such hope for any form of future security. One of my closest women friends informed me recently that at thirteen her most faithful childhood companion, a Chinese girl who lived two floors down in the same apartment building in Kuala Lumpur, suddenly stopped coming over to play because her parents had sold her body and her time to an old man at whose sexual beck and call she was now obliged to exist. My friend, playing hopscotch alone on the sidewalk, would watch her leave home every day, aloof and instantly older, for her assignation in another part of town.

If unbeknownst to me other girls were being forced into a simulacrum of womanhood in the twinkling of an old man's eye, my own progress in the field was causing me to come to some rather curious conclusions. From haphazard readings from my parents' bookcase I had gathered a vague and paradoxical idea that the height of sexual passion would somehow involve an out-of-body experience, that one would in some way lose consciousness and become vulnerable to all physical danger, as if aspiring to contemplate the face of God while on a roller coaster. As my development then stood, real life was much more seductive, much too grippingly real for me to aspire to any such dubious adventures. So my view of sex existed only in outline, like an artist's initial sketch of a nude: something to be blocked in, the details finished later. For instance, a woman doctor who had come to school to talk to us girls about sex, mostly about the road to pregnancy, explained to us that *out of the blue* one's husband's penis would be inserted into one's vagina (cold, anatomical terms, incidentally, we had never heard pronounced until that very moment, although we had of course seen them in print, such was the general silence on the matter). She then informed us there would be a sudden explosion of semen, and that would suddenly, miraculously and (such was the godlike omnipotence of manhood) *of itself* cause us to conceive. All this did not sound particularly appealing. And, although the good doctor had made the part about insertion very clear, she omitted to tell us that the virile member would previously have undergone an engorgement of blood leading to something called an erection. This led some of the more mechanically minded among us to wonder how such a trick as insertion could possibly be performed in the first place.

When I reached the fifth form, I was seventeen and had little time for tenuous conjectures. In any case, some of my more foggy misapprehensions had already been dispelled. David had left for Pakistan to study toward a degree in veterinary science, and it was expected to be years before I saw him again. Although I had been in a state of utter denial before his departure (not to mention stunned by the fact there was a world beyond ours where he could possibly find himself at home), his absence left a profound fissure: an abyss whose depths no amount of activity provided by the ever increasing demands of school and social life managed to lessen. As life itself seemed to have stopped, I stopped writing in my diary. The year was 1965. When hostilities broke out between India and Pakistan, a constant, riveting fear for his safety took over. When he came home for good in mid-December, we felt as if nothing could ever possibly come between us again. Nevertheless, things were never quite the same for us.

In retrospect, I believe that David, who was nearly two years older than I, returned having gained much more maturity from his few months' experience abroad than was matched by my progress at home in his absence. We continued to be happy together, united by a sense of belonging. But things were beginning to change in our friends and our surroundings, imperceptibly at first and then in ways that dropped the tiniest seeds of suspicion regarding disturbing realities about my peers. They were losing the delighted candor of before, reaching a stage that was harsher, more predatory in its finality. Their identities had taken shape. They were playing for keeps.

I wanted no part of it. I loved the beautiful fluidity of my own world too much: its sense of promise, the knowledge that things divine were still to be revealed before me. In the face of the soul-abrading challenges befalling many of the young people I knew, only language seemed real to me. Through language I had sought to reach an inviolable closeness with the people that surrounded me, to expunge the very visible fact I was not born one of them. Language and a closely guarded public image, since I knew that any slip on my part would be noticed and discussed immediately, bringing my expatriate status into sharp focus and setting back by countless, agonizing steps any progress in my desperate quest to belong. Language, however, was my friend: it was protean and pliable and could encompass all manner of alluring blandishments. Through language my desire for love could be safe from public scrutiny. But this longing that I had labored to fashion into the poetry of shared speech was heard mainly, as I failed to understand at the time, as a background of normality against which something more concrete was expected to take place.

However, at this point, I was acutely attuned to the voice, manner and general aura of everyone I met. I would steal surreptitious, intense glances at people who passed by in the streets, who sat near me in restaurants, who stood in line with me for the movies, plumbing, always plumbing the depths of their souls through the well of their words. When I answered the telephone, my ears sucked up the slightest vocal idiosyncrasy. As I gabbled away to invisible friends, my mother always knew by my inflection whether my interlocutor was a native Malay, Indian, Cantonese or Hokkien speaker. I read books in the same way, pulsing to the narrator's idiolect, straining every sense to grasp hold of something in the voice. But what exactly? I fell in love with voices – what they said, how they said it, what they might have chosen to omit – and, above all, with the suspension points that in my mind always trailed behind them. I was convinced that Malaysians were speaking in celestial tongues and I was missing the meaning of life.

But where was my sense of self in all this? I was on the brink of consolidating my young womanhood, no longer an outsider in my own world. I was acquiring a certain aura of my own, and it was known that a rather brooding younger colleague of my father's had mentioned to my parents that he was waiting for me to grow up so he could marry me.

One evening, as I was musing in one of the teak-framed easy chairs in our Kuala Lumpur living room, I was plunged into a mysterious atmosphere of white sands, straw hats and calypso music. 'Ah, bliss!' I thought, adding for the benefit of no one in particular, 'Wouldn't it be lovely to live in Jamaica?'

'That's interesting,' said my father without turning a hair. 'We're actually leaving next month. Everything's been arranged for weeks. By the way, how did you know?'

It was a fait accompli, the next step in my father's career and my family's travels. There was no point in protesting. We called the packers in.

Our final send-off at Kuala Lumpur airport as we left Malaysia for parts foreign was impressive and strangely perplexing. It was attended by motley representatives of every tangent of my parents' presence in the land, plus several very unexpected people we had not really counted among our friends. As it was a school day, none of my friends was present except – unexpectedly – David, who had decided at the last minute to call in sick at the Victoria Institution. A kind of confused, tentative gaiety stumbled around us. The senders-off seemed to be expecting a party, although none of them knew each other well enough to be convivial. I sensed an underlying touch of grimness in the chatter of some of our expatriate friends – the Evanses were 'going home' ('getting out', some Americans harshly called it) – now that Malayanization was the order of the day and Europeans might soon be welcome no longer. Many of our friends had already bid us farewell with parties, gifts, speeches and, in my case, a fabulous Chinese banquet organized by my classmates at an elegant hotel. David and I had parted stoically, refusing to let unswerving reality crash-land into our hearts.

Laden with last-minute presents and with the goodbyes of our friends still ringing in my ears, I was finally accommodated on the BOAC flight. I found that I had a window seat next to a podgy, still sweating Eastern European man. My parents and John were sitting together across the aisle. I was grateful to be separated from them. I wept deeply and quietly. I was nevertheless conscious of the fact that events would outrun me swiftly enough and I would soon be swept along in the spate of rivers yet unnamed, my thrashing limbs falling with each stroke into the ever more regular, recognizable movements of the optimistic swimmer. But, looking down at the Malay Peninsula from the plane's oval window, I knew there was nothing that could be done, I should weep out my heart's elegy for David, my language, the way my world was configured through it, my friends and the comfort of the homely fascinations I was leaving behind. It was unquestionable, even to me, that nothing could have stayed the hand of that particular fate. Life would happen in spite of it. I would soon forget.

The author at the beach in Jamaica in 1967.

2 ISLAND GIRL?

I'm sad to say I'm on my way
Won't be back for many a day
My heart is down, my head is turning around
I had to leave a little girl in Kingston town

                                    Irving Burgie, 'Jamaica Farewell'

There is no point in describing the few watershed months we spent in Britain at my grandmother's house before sailing to Jamaica, where my father would take up his position at the University of the West Indies at Kingston: the usual frustrations of letter writing and expecting, the usual resumption of sporadic, optimistic reconnoitering sessions with beloved relatives of my mother's, her own distressed sense of displacement, my father's abstraction in his work, my brother's loneliness. Our arrival in Kingston dispelled the hothouse memories of what family life in Britain had invariably become for John and me: an existence in a capsule, suffocating because we inevitably lacked the time, experience and wherewithal to create with the rest of the British Isles a reality beyond our walls. And what we had absorbed from books as our heritage was a fairy tale, of no practical use and reflecting no current reality.

But Jamaica provided us with a different set of realities, some in dimensions we had not expected. Parallel to the sense of not quite existing in the physical universe around me was the fact that our university bungalow was inhabited by a duppy. The day we arrived in Kingston, two members of my father's department came to meet us off the boat and drive us to our new home. I rode with my brother in one car with the guarded young academic who was to be our neighbor while my parents were borne off in another. It was a beautiful, bright day, and we were excited at having arrived and optimistic about our new life in Jamaica. As we approached our designated home, our neighbor said, 'I hope you like ghosts, Carys.' When I answered that I was indeed interested in them, he responded nonchalantly, 'Just as well, you've got the campus haunted house!'

I was appalled at this news, mainly for prudish reasons. For hours I didn't dare go to the bathroom for fear of the ghost's possible pruriency and, even when I caved in under the realization that three years was going to be too long a time to cross one's legs, I did so clenching my teeth in embarrassment. The following day, I mentioned to my mother what the neighbor had disclosed.

'Well,' she said thoughtfully. 'It sounds like a poltergeist from what Alan said. We'll know for sure when our china arrives. In the meantime, we'll get a dog. Dogs can always tell if there's a ghost about. And, if there is, it might be a friendly one, you never know.'

The author with her mother and brother in the garden of their haunted house in Kingston in 1968.

The author and a neighbor in Kingston in 1968.

63 ~ Island Girl?

Nothing happened for a year. Then one day as I was getting ready to go out, a bottle of hardened glue on the table in my bedroom jumped about six inches into the air, gave a little waggle and set itself down again. Horrified and dismayed, I said a little prayer to defend myself against any evil and checked to see if anything else in the room had moved. Nothing had. I went out to the living room to let my mother know what had happened.

'Either I'm going mad or there's a ghost in the house after all,' I told her. Her answer did not include the reassurance about my sanity that I had assumed it would.

'Well, darling, you *have* been a bit overwrought lately. What with the move to a new country, all the work you did for the O levels, being made a prefect at St Hugh's, it wouldn't surprise me at all if your nerves weren't what they ought to be.'

Well, thanks a bunch! I put the glue bottle out of my mind, watching myself to see if I was in fact losing my marbles. But – and not quite to my relief – I seemed much the same as ever. A few weeks later, I was to experience something that struck me at the time as very unusual. I was sitting at my sewing machine one twilight, putting together a fashionable new tent dress I had cut from a beautiful piece of batik I'd found. The sewing machine had a sloping, roof-shaped cover with a suitcase-type handle and was on the floor, diagonally opposite the left-hand corner of my table. I could not see the cover from where I sat. Suddenly I heard a loud, repeated, rattle-like thumping from the general direction of the cover. Suspecting that one of the many house lizards that ran across the walls had somehow got in underneath it and was banging its tail in an attempt to get out – something that had occasionally happened when they crept under pictures on the wall – I skipped off to fetch my father to do the honors and shake the poor, trapped thing from the box. My father manfully shook the box, looked inside and pronounced that it must have got away. Relieved, I went back to the sewing machine and resumed my sewing.

After a minute or two, I heard the same thumping from the cover of the sewing machine. Cautiously I got up from my chair and crept around the table to a position from which I could observe the box. I was astonished to see the handle, apparently of its own accord, flinging itself from side to side of the box, creating the racket that had caught my attention before.

I have always considered what followed to be the culminating moment of my life. Never again will I be able to process so many thoughts so fast in succession, never again will I be able to remain so calm in such an emergency, nor make such a wise decision. I thought to myself, 'I don't know whether ghosts exist. If they exist, it's better not to antagonize them. On the other hand, it's also best not to give in to them. One should be firm, but kind, as with dogs. If you run screaming from this room now, you will never be able to enter it again. Say something firm. Just in case they exist.' Excruciatingly aware of how ludicrous I would have looked to a casual observer, I forced myself to address the box – just in case, of course.

'Why don't you help me for a change, instead of frightening me all the time,' I said in a would-be humorous voice. *Mano de santo*, as the Spanish would say. It certainly did the trick. The banging stopped. I went back to get on with my sewing, but, just as my rear end was about to reach the seat of the chair, the electric sewing machine began to run by itself. I had not had time to touch the material, much less to steer it under the needle in a straight seam. Nevertheless, at top speed the machine sewed a straight line exactly where I had intended to sew – an impossibility if there is no guiding hand to keep the fabric straight. This went on for several inches before I completely lost my head. 'Stop!' I screamed, utterly out of my depth. 'Stop!'

The sewing did not stop until I began to kick the table legs, and there ensued a silence the like of which I have never experienced again. It's not often that a spirit calls one's bluff. I had to believe now – no 'just in case' about it.

The following day, I had a powwow with my mother as to what to do about the poltergeist. I suggested bringing in a Catholic priest and having it sorted out. We weren't Catholics, but we'd all read enough to understand they had powers of exorcism. My mother demurred.

'What if we send it to a worse place than this?' she asked. 'We don't want that.'

I agreed.

'Has it done you any actual harm? I mean, has it been aggressive towards you in any way?'

It had not.

'Tell you what,' said my mother. 'Let's not mess with it, on the understanding that, the minute it starts throwing ink bottles at you or flings books through the air or anything, we'll call in the priest. How's that?'

So we agreed to let it stay as long as it behaved itself. And it did behave itself, more or less. It sometimes changed my toiletries around from one side of the dressing table to the other and was once actually seen by my mother moving a bottle of scent as she passed the door on her way up the long corridor. If anything was mislaid, we would laugh it off, saying 'Oh, Josephine must have been playing with it. It'll show up soon enough!' Josephine was the name we had given the entity after an inquisitorial session with the Ouija board divulged it to be a fourteen-year-old girl of that name who had died, it was to be surmised, in the hospital on the ground where the house now stood. She had also done my mother a favor by transporting the book she was reading up the corridor from the living room to my parents' bedroom while my mother took a shower. Josephine had left the book open at a different page, though, the careless thing.

When we began to mention Josephine to our friends people were very surprised at our phlegm. 'Oh, you English are so brave!' gushed one lady from Martinique, oblivious to the fact that we were not one of us English. 'I would have moved out *immediately*!' Our protestations that Josephine was nobody to be afraid of didn't convince the woman one bit. 'Well, do be careful!' she warned. 'You know what happened to the Manleys!'

It transpired that the Manleys, part of a well-known Jamaican political family, had had a very rough time indeed in the house. Once, after a weekend in the country, they returned to a revolting stench coming from the kitchen. This turned out to be a line of packages of rotting meat that had been taken out of the refrigerator and placed in a chain along the ten-foot-long kitchen counter. The poltergeist must have been fascinated by that counter, for on another occasion, we were told, it rustled up all Carmen Manley's considerable costume jewelry from various caches in the house and made a similar chain with it. This was discovered the morning after attending a certain party, when the Manleys blamed one of their friends for the event – a friend who had had too much to drink at the party and been offered a bed for the night on the living-room sofa. The hung-over friend was accused by Carmen Manley of betraying her hospitality and rummaging among her drawers. Other occasions were described to us, concerning strange men's shoes under Mrs Manley's bed and pots and pans all over the garden. The Manleys eventually moved out, and the next occupants had experienced unexplained incidents too, but none as shocking as the Manleys had.

Vincent, who tended to our garden every Monday, once revealed to me that every week, when he showed up for work, he would find his gardening tools scattered all over our one-acre yard despite the fact he always put them away where our maid Doris' grandchildren couldn't get at them. Not only that, he added, but, when he lay down for a nap after lunch in our garage (my father was not supposed to know this part of the story, Vincent was being paid by the hour), he could feel an invisible woman snuggling down beside him and blowing in his ear. When told about Josephine, he was somewhat mollified. Randy fourteen-year-old girls were one thing, I realized, unnamable presences were quite another.

Beyond the confines of our beautiful, shaded bungalow lay a holographic nation with a repertoire of vastly contradictory scenes that flashed into view according to how you moved the picture and then disappeared again just as quickly. Jamaica is an island of striking natural beauty, with enough of a dashing past to splash the travel brochures with romance: the Blue Mountains, the dazzling white beaches, the waterfalls, the higglers' markets heaving with noisily cheerful country folk selling colorful straw hats and succulent tropical fruits, Jamaica where da rum com from, the Jamaica of smiling natives, calypso music, Harry Belafonte. Punctuate this relaxing scene with flashes of Spanish galleons, buccaneers, Sir Henry Morgan, pieces of eight, and you will have a Jamaica that is the creation of an excellent public relations bureau. The Jamaica I remember was racked with the sort of unemployment that brings devastating poverty and demoralization and, shockingly, hatred and cruelty among Jamaicans themselves. Men with eyes bleary from hunger lived within sight and sound of hotels where private planes are part of the daily service and a guest's culinary caprices could be flown in for dinner from any part of the world. The smiling, suave young waiter bearing the cocktail-in-a-coconut to the promotional-flyer tourist had often just stepped from a scene of Hogarthian wretchedness. Many people had no shoes, some had literally only the shirt on their backs, often children missed school if their clothes had not dried in time after a rainstorm. *The Daily Gleaner* and the evening newspaper regularly ran stories of murders committed over an article of clothing. One countrywoman, when asked why she had agreed to move in with a man who abused her regularly, had answered simply, 'He gave me a pair of boots.'

For the first time in my life, I was physically afraid of other people. Everything I saw suggested that people would hate me for my skin color, my straight hair, my privileged life, and knife me for anything I had on. Although I was only in physical danger once, when a teenage boy on a bicycle jumped on me as I took a shortcut across campus – a terrifying event that caused me to tremble for years afterward whenever I chanced to be alone with an unknown male in the same street or elevator – I learned to be very wary when out of the house. The carefully fostered illusion of a color-blind island existed within the hotels – mainly at their private beaches and poolside, from which tourists were not encouraged to wander – and abroad. Jamaica in the sixties seethed with racial tension, a society strangled not only within the binary black-versus-white scenario, but also between each shade and visible ethnic trait of those two poles. Soon after our arrival, a wealthy, white, Jamaican-born woman who owned a great deal of land in the countryside was assaulted, bound to a chair and tortured by people who had not been content just to rob her. The ideals of the Black Panthers ignited a fire fueled by revenge for centuries of humiliation and economic devastation in the face of blatant wealth. The notion of black power ran so deeply counter to ingrained Jamaican reality that to some it must have seemed as revolutionary as Copernicus' idea of a round world. The hatred was palpable as one walked the streets of Kingston. It was certainly not necessary to read the graffiti that screamed out 'Black Christmas this December!'

The top socioeconomic level of the country was not only clearly white-dominated, but some of its members appeared to be fresh out of Hampshire. Many of the old planter families tended to marry English or American spouses to keep the Caucasian gene pool in fresh supply. The rest of the island's inhabitants fared monetarily and socially in blatant descending order of whiteness; if possible, people tried to marry whiter. Color meant everything, and it was no use pretending otherwise. Only the Rastafarians valued their own negritude. Everybody else, at least in the city, was a potential predator or saw themselves as an exploitable artistic commodity. People did the cruelest things to those struggling to get ahead. My brother once wrote down the story of the Orchid Man, who would cycle down from the mountains every few weeks to bring my mother and other people we knew a very few, exquisite orchids from which they would generally select one to buy. He adored his orchids, and they were his only means of making a little money. One day he came down to our yard in tears: somebody had viciously destroyed all his orchid plants, he now had absolutely nothing in the world, no means of making even the most basic living for himself. He was devastated.

As I write it becomes clear that a great part of my rejection of the Jamaican experience was directly due to the fact that it had thrown a great deal of life's dirty laundry directly into my lap. Had I received a more ordinary, curate's-egg childhood ('only rotten in parts, madam, the rest is quite good!'), the island would not have provoked the same sense of revulsion, and the many delightful people and inspiring experiences I enjoyed there would have impinged more prominently on my consciousness of it. However, I had lived through Malaysia in a state of mental grace, shown and seeing only that which was beautiful and good.

It did not take the family very long to realize that our accumulated experience in Malaysia was about as relevant in the West Indies as a sandcastle moat in a monsoon. Nothing we knew could be recycled. We were no longer 'Europeans', people from one more of the world's cultures mingling with the existing community. We were 'White', and that's all we were. It was useless to behave in accordance with one's old habits when one knew oneself exonerated in advance of any suspicion of malice regarding color and culture, all disclaimers unnecessary. Color in Jamaica was the axle around which too many social relations turned. Since it was assumed that in any interpersonal association color would be foremost in one's mind, for us it was forced to become so. One evening at a campus film night, I was talking with some rather aloof undergraduates I had just met. The subject got around to race relations, and one of the young men mentioned something about 'the climate of mutual distrust' that existed between blacks and whites on the island. I was shaken. *Mutual* distrust? It was hard to be told that people mistrusted me because of my ethnicity and even harder to realize there exist historical forces that will seal your fate despite your good intentions as a blameless individual. It's one thing to be indignant about what one reads in history books, quite another to be caught between clashing tides.

The intricate origins of Jamaican self-hatred became very real to me during those three years in Kingston. At school, I learned the mechanics of how West Africans were sold into the English slave trade, often by kinsmen well versed in these dealings from having sold slaves to other Africans, and brought to the West Indies and America on the infamous Middle Passage, whose horrors were faithfully described in drawn cross-sections of individual ships. The story of what later happened to the captives is well known, but no less shaming. Suffice it to say that the planters' policy of breaking up groups of speakers of the same language so that no united bands could form to plot the overthrow of the masters also had the longer-term effect of dissolving any sense of group identity. A result of this was that many elements of different African cultures were eradicated also, and people were left to piece together a new set of mores out of scraps of both European and African West Indian customs. In later years, however, slave rebellions were formed under outstanding leaders, and the Maroons – Cimarrons, runaway slaves who formed their own community in the mountains – are legendary to this day. Mainly, however, Jamaican negritude entailed poverty, a broken spirit, a broken sense of self even side by side with hatred of the white oppressor and, in many cases, a conviction of white moral superiority.

The idea of white *moral* superiority shocked me to the core. Technological superiority – well, yes, obviously. But *moral*? I had somehow sensed that if anybody were to feel morally superior it would be the slaves. Then again, I was laboring under the apprehension that the West Indian slaves, at least the first generations, considered their condition to be extraordinary – something inflicted upon blacks by whites – when in fact African black-on-black slavery was a common phenomenon. Was it recognition of a superior, in the sense of more powerful, community that caused these feelings of inferiority? Also, what is moral inferiority? Whose morals are to be the yardstick? I was to hear constant declarations from poor black people about the superiority of whites. One startling example was provided one day by our live-in maid, Doris. A cheerful woman in her fifties, she was struggling to take care of an often fluctuating number of smallish children. Two of these 'picknies', as she called them, were her own grandchildren, whom she was rearing until their mother, a recent emigrant to

Britain, could afford to send for them. Although we had been advised by all sorts of people not to allow them to live on the premises, we saw no reason why they should not, and so two or three children stayed with Doris in the two rooms, bathroom and tiny kitchen that made up the maid's quarters. Other children often in attendance were the offspring her companion of many years, Mr Johnson, had fathered with another, younger woman, but we never got to know this group very well as they seemed to change constantly. Doris was great company and a repository of all kinds of island lore. She was convinced that the sooner the children were sent to their mothers, the better. The picknies' leaving of the home island to face alienation in the gray dampness and cold of England was a sacrifice that had to be faced if the children were to have a chance at any kind of future. Her reasons surprised me.

'Why's that, Doris?'

'Lah an' ahder, Miss Kya,' she answered at once. 'Lah an' ahder.'

She did not elaborate, but I think Doris meant that Britain would afford her grandchildren a place where they could see it was possible to earn a living without fear of being robbed at machete point and, perhaps just as importantly, where crime brought swift retribution. Doris was always afraid that, if left in Jamaica, the grandsons would grow up to be 'rude boys'. Also, thanks to the British welfare state, she could be sure they would be fed if they fell on hard times, something that was tragically impossible in Jamaica. Meanwhile, the two boys played around the yard, often chased by a broom-wielding Doris, were taken to the Kingston Hospital emergency room whenever necessary, and celebrated their birthdays and other festive occasions when they came along. Sadly, however, we were all much too involved in our own worries to concern ourselves too much with playing with the boys: as they were both under six, they were somewhat beneath my brother's notice as playmates. It took Fred D'Aguiar's book *Dear Future*, which I read almost thirty years later, to reveal the misery and sense of abandonment those little boys must have been suffering as they waited for their mother to take them with her.

One day, I was in the kitchen, giggling with Doris about our next-door neighbor, who had been reported in the local press as having been caught by the police in a pair of blue-and-white striped underpants with a young woman not his wife. My mother later explained to me that, since adultery would have to be proven in order for his wife to be able to divorce him (there was no such thing then as no-fault divorce), he had taken the common expedient of arranging to be caught with a prostitute. The reason he wanted a divorce was in order to marry another woman with whom he had been having a rather noisy affair, but it was not a question of disgracing her: the deed had to be done through a professional. There were girls who specialized in this, I was told. They would undertake to play cards with you all night until the police put in an appearance. (Be that as it may, I never caught sight of that poor, dispirited neighbor again without thinking about the then novelty of his blue-and-white striped underpants.) In any case, I was telling Doris all about the incident, which seemed to me just about the juiciest news that could possibly fall into our laps. However, I was quite unprepared for Doris' reaction.

'Lard, Miss Kya, I never know white people do dat!'
'Do what, Doris?'
'Sleep with other people wife!'
'Why not?'
'Because dey better than we!'

Try as I might to get her to qualify what she had just said, Doris remained adamant in her belief that black people were more depraved than whites. She must have had ample opportunity in her long years as a domestic aide in the houses of white folks to discover that this was not true, so her attitude was astonishing. But its corollary was not lost on me either. This meant that black people need not worry themselves too much about behaving: what was the point if they were no good to start with? An isolated conversation should not engender an entire theory of Jamaican social life and attitudes, but the revelation shook me enough to consider some of the ramifications of self-hatred and how it inevitably leads to the hatred of those who are like oneself. This explained to some degree the acts of great cruelty poorer Jamaicans often inflicted on each other. I say 'to some degree' because there was starvation and consequently anger and frustration to consider also, and were these not enough? The idea of inherent black sexual immorality, however, was a puzzler. The ruling white discourse on the subject, as I was forced to garner from the number of times it was related to me, ran along the following lines. Back in slavery days, the slave owners needed as many hands as possible to work the sugar plantations as cheaply as possible. So they encouraged the male slaves to make as many women pregnant as they could so that the masters wouldn't have to buy extra workers. The female slaves didn't mind because the more children they had, the more prized they were and the more privileges they received. Being fruitful was their only pride. And the more children the men fathered, the more their reputation blossomed as big men on the plantation. Now the male slaves didn't have to worry about feeding their children because the slave owners would take care of it. So they got into the habit of having more and more children and never asking whether they or the mothers needed anything. That is why so many Jamaicans are so promiscuous today and why there are so many starving children running around whose mothers have forgotten which child was by which father. And that is why no Jamaican father believes he has responsibility for feeding and rearing his kids. Only now there are no slave owners to do it for them, but the men still haven't figured this out.

Every middle-class person I knew, black or white, seemed to believe this version of history. Many years later, I came to read accounts of US plantation society in which the above version of things was thrown into quite different perspective. Firstly, some of the West African communities were matriarchal: at the very least, women enjoyed enough authority to be able to decide for themselves when and with whom they would engage in sexual relations. (In the Caribbean and the US, of course, rape and other pressures from white slave owners would add another factor to the mix later on.) The men were not expected to concern themselves particularly with the feeding of the children since young ones were considered as belonging to the women and their upbringing a matter for the community as a whole: it took a village to raise the children. Therefore, the family dynamic was as structurally different from the European tradition as it could possibly be. Female sexual autonomy and male freedom from child-rearing were then pitted against the prevailing Protestant mores and found not only wanting, but actively immoral and unchristian. However, the slaves' previous social structures went unrecognized and, if it is true that history reflects the viewpoint of the victors, it is no less certain that dominant ideas of morality reflect the values of the powerful.

Oblivious to its historical underpinnings, I continued to be fascinated by Doris' own story. For over thirty years, she had had a companion whom she would not marry, for she considered him a terrible loser. However, she fed his children by the other woman he actually lived with. When I asked her why she wouldn't marry Mr Johnson, as she invariably referred to him, she told me that marriage was a very important thing, one didn't go around marrying just anyone and Mr Johnson had too many girlfriends.

'Then why did you have so many children with him, Doris, if you thought he wasn't good enough for you?'

'Because he 'ad good hair,' replied Doris mysteriously.

Indeed, Mr Johnson, some of whose ancestors were from India by way of Trinidad, was partly Indian and had straight hair – or rather curly hair of non-African origin. This had once made him a great prize among the ladies, Doris told me, but he had later spoiled his hair by not keeping it covered while working for a while as a house painter.

I found it hard to understand Doris' reasons, which seemed entirely frivolous. But then I had never had to fight for every crust in a world where those with non-black features had the advantage and I had never had to think about the effects of this on my children's survival. There was no question at the time of admiring a distinct black aesthetic: Grace Knight had not yet made her mark. Black was ugly, which explains the explosive emotional reaction to the movement that screamed out to millions that 'Black was Beautiful'.

There was a girl in my class at St Hugh's, Alice, who had known this for years. She was a taciturn Rastafarian, tall and strong with what later came to be called a very short afro, and she stood out against the other black senior girls, who wore their hair primly straightened and coifed and dreaded playing sports for the havoc that perspiration would wreak at their hairlines. They spent a great deal of their time outside school with their hair in rollers, which created in itself a sexy aesthetic that was considered far better than appearing *au naturel*. Although all the black men were unabashed about their African hair, their sisters worked endlessly to circumvent public viewings of unstraightened hair, and any inadvertent showing of it brought forth nervous giggles, as if something risqué were involved. People blushed at the mere mention of it, rather in the same way I had blushed when told, many years later by a radical German colleague who years earlier had participated in the European May of 1968, that some women students had shown up buck-naked for a classics lecture at her tradition-bound university. Back in Jamaica, at about the same time, a furor had been caused by a television ad for Sunsilk shampoo in which a woman with fine, air-flying, long blond hair had run languorously along a beach of white sands in slow motion. Local women had flocked to buy the product, believing that it would transform their own hair into silken tresses of spun gold, only to be enraged at what they felt was a scam. The events following the ad, which had been released on an ethnocentric premise that the customer already had hair very like that of the model on the beach (the company promised no transracial miracles), pointed all too painfully to the longing experienced by many of the island women to possess straight, or at least wavy, hair.

Alice could not have given a monkey's toss for such considerations, which she considered pandering to white supremacy. As far as she was concerned, there was nothing to be embarrassed about in the way she was put together and people should have more sense than to worry about trying not to look overly black. This revolutionary stance was rather too avant-garde for most girls in the class. Apart from one or two close friends, people kept away from Alice, although she clearly commanded great respect. One day, in the washroom, I was lamenting to the world in general about my somewhat chubby tummy, which I considered a curse and out of proportion with the rest of myself. Two sinks away, Alice surprised me by answering my remark. She had never bothered much with me or with any of the humanities stream girls for that matter.

'Woman must 'ave belly,' she boomed irrefutably. 'Man like woman to 'ave belly.'

This was definitely a friendly gesture, though I was thrown by her earthiness. She was merely imparting information, not attempting to bond. Bonding with the likes of me was not Alice's thing. Alice was the only girl in the school who refused to speak standard Jamaican English in class. There were other things she refused to do as well. It was customary on rainy sports days to forego the usual games in favor of calisthenics or, very occasionally, folk dancing indoors. One day, the gym teacher announced that we were going to learn the Highland fling. She got out a gramophone and record and set the needle down on the revolving disk, instructing us meanwhile to find partners. When a friend turned to Alice, she was told with great simplicity and even greater conviction, 'I won't dance no white man's dance.'

The Highland fling, a white man's dance! I was stunned. It was a *Scottish* dance!

While the rest of us galumphed around the gym, Alice stood on the sidelines, quietly watching. The teacher did not insist on her participation in this spectacle, which was beginning to look more and more unseemly. It was the first time I had seen a superior's orders defied with impunity. The sky had not fallen, there had been no unpleasantness.

The Highland fling came back to haunt me a few years later, at York University. A particularly conservative, upper-crust acquaintance of mine was celebrating his twenty-first birthday and had invited me to a rather exclusive party. The affair had seemed to be quite civilized until the Gay Gordons was announced. This, it turned out, was a highly energetic, organized dance done to preset patterns and steps, which everybody else seemed to know. I did my disheveled best, my partner pushing me very hard and very obviously where I was supposed to go. This was followed by the St Bernard's Waltz (a truly inane exercise), the Military Two-Step (which involved the men saluting smartly and clicking their heels together every half minute while the ladies curtsied at them) and the aforementioned 'Heeland fleng'. It soon became clear that, in certain British circles, lack of familiarity with these dances was social suicide, like professing a dislike of cricket. But the Highland fling was still being taught at Jamaican girls' schools in the sixties, and Alice may have been the first student to protest.

Too overwhelmed by those Caribbean years, I tried everything I could to expunge them from memory. But I retain a ragbag of memories, some of them happy ones, others benchmarks of grief. One of the happier memories was a visit to a classmate's pig farm in the country outside Kingston. My friend Anne Johnson invited me to stay for a few days. Our time was spent, for me at least, in bucolic bliss, visiting Anne's kindly relatives all over the village, attending the tiny chapel with its fiery revivalist songs, being taken for a tour of the pigs, paying our respects at Anne's grandmother's grave under a tree in their yard. Everyone seemed pleased to see me, nobody seemed resentful of my presence, although there were very few young people, a given in rural areas in those days. The whole experience was like something out of a soothing reader for children from the late nineteenth century. There was only one television in the whole village, installed just over a year before in the local bar. It was said to have already played an enormous role in lowering the community birth rate.

I dated a few young men, most of them students of one kind or another, but I would generally get sick of being shown around as a trophy. Island customs didn't help one's sense of self either:

sometimes guys would arrange to pick me up for a party at a certain time and not show up for three hours. They would gripe because I was no longer interested in going out. My father could never quite believe this was going on. 'He might have broken his leg,' he responded one evening, when I was particularly angry at being made to wait. 'How do you know he hasn't been in an accident?' But I did have great times with other young beaux, dancing the weekends away at outdoor jump-ups and parties in friends' houses. I loved the music of Jamaica. First it was ska, then reggae – reggae hopping, hiccupping always, everywhere. It was the music of survival.

Young people's parties were very different from what my parents were now attending. According to my mother, these were dreadfully boring events at which a strangely marked type of sexual segregation was clearly enforced. The only women dancing were the unmarried or divorced ones; all married women were abandoned by the male guests, who were either drinking together in groups or dancing with the unmarried women. The matrons, therefore, were obliged to sit about in brave clusters, talking grimly about domestic issues and trying not to be caught squinting out of the corner of their eyes at their possibly straying husbands. There was no chance of mixed conversation at all. I invariably found myself either dancing with a man or talking with the women. Sometimes a married man would offer to give his dancing partner a ride home, and one could only guess at the scene that might or might not erupt when he finally arrived at his own home. Adult relationships seemed utilitarian, to say the least. But grown-ups were also now seen to be making convenient exceptions, reversing the policies on which I had been raised, juggling the figures that led up to the sum total of my previous reality.

The parties my parents threw seemed more in line with what

I had seen adults do in the past, although I was usually too busy with my own social life to want to attend. One Sunday, I came home mid-afternoon – in time, I had calculated, to help tidy up after a drinks party my parents had put on before lunch. The bungalow was still teeming with people, although cars were beginning to crawl down the driveway and you could tell the affair was thinning out. As I stepped onto the front patio, a middle-aged woman with mid-brown, indifferently permed hair stumbled out of our still noisy living room on her way to her car. I caught her just in time to save her from falling face down on the hard green tiles. It was Caroline Williams, the British-born wife of Henry Williams, a well-known Jamaican academic from the island's white elite. He was also a famous philanderer.

'Hello, Carys dear!' she mumbled drunkenly, trying to beam roguishly at me. 'Where have you been?'

As I attempted to prevent this sweet and loving mother of one of my closest friends from lurching out of my grasp, I could see my own mother hurrying out to help me, signaling frantically for me to go inside. But it was too late. I had already noticed that Mrs Williams had tucked a white cocktail napkin into her décolletage.

'Oh, look, you've written yourself a note!' I pointed out helpfully, leaning over to retrieve it.

'It's all right, darling, I'll look after things here!' interrupted my mother in a determined voice. 'Why don't you go inside and help Doris round up the empty glasses?'

However, I had already seen the writing on the napkin. In large, uppercase letters, at some point during the party, Mrs Williams had inked in the following legend: 'I MUST BE LOSING MY FLAVOUR'.

During the days that followed, I gave a lot of thought to that napkin. There was no way on God's earth any of us could have brushed the incident aside as trivial. We could only pray that Caroline and everybody else had been far too drunk to remember what had happened and she would have no clue as to the innumerably devastating ways in which she had humiliated herself.

It was weeks before I dared to go and see her daughter, Samantha, again and, when I did, I struggled with my secret burden of being privy to her mother's shame. As Mrs Williams, smiling kindly as ever, brought us pop and cookies from the kitchen, I saw that at least outwardly she had slipped back into her matronly role as if nothing had happened. But if Samantha's ostensibly solid family was undermined by such insidious truths as her father's infidelities and her mother's fragile vulnerability, what could be happening to adults all around me? They were certainly starting to show me the seams that held their authority together. Albeit unwittingly, Caroline Williams had even invited me to help unpick them.

The idea that the kind of grown-ups we knew were people who, having survived adolescence, had therefore sorted themselves out in a more or less civilized manner was another concept that fell apart all too quickly during those Jamaican days. Kingston seemed to be bristling with people, usually expatriates, who held outrageously barbaric views and saw no reason to tune them down. Some of them lived in faculty housing too. One evening, an Englishwoman whose husband taught anthropology came over to borrow a cup of sugar. My mother didn't know her well, although she knew she had several small children. She offered her a chair on the veranda and a cool drink. The usual pleasantries were going well enough, so my mother, who had noticed that the woman was heavily pregnant, asked her when her baby was due.

'Oh, not for a couple of weeks,' answered the woman happily.

'We already have four, and they're quite a handful, but, as Richard says, it's important that superior people like us have as many babies as we can – to even things out, you know.'

I wasn't there to hear my mother's answer, but the woman never came over again. 'Bloody master-race types!' my mother fumed to me later. 'That daft cow couldn't find her nose with a powder puff!' The last thing my mother had expected to find in Jamaica was a quisling, although more Hitler sympathizers were to emerge among our neighbors. One of these, a whiskery old academic known to me as Mr Newcroft, kept trying to get my parents to come over and listen to his collection of Hitler's greatest speeches. I was astonished that university lecturers could be Fascist sympathizers and was not surprised when I heard the Newcrofts had a regular burglar who limited him or herself to stealing just *one* out of a pair of Mrs Newcroft's dainty little *Übermensch* shoes.

It was at St Hugh's that I studied for my O levels, failing only in Art. I had been advised not to sit for the Math exam since I would certainly fail it and I took a newly introduced, lower-level math certification instead. (I have no idea what this certification was aimed to show; I overheard one teacher tell another the exam must have been a pushover if even Carys managed to pass it!) In my final year, I was made Head Girl – a huge honor within the British school system and one that brought with it the responsibility of certain ceremonial duties and of running the group of elite prefects. I was later told, though, that there had been protests from some teachers that the nomination would appear to be racially motivated. The headmistress, Mrs Carnegie, had apparently won the day by saying that it certainly would be racially motivated if anybody else were named to the position. Affirmative action had not yet been thought of. But I don't think I was a stellar Head Girl. There was a close classmate I thought would have done things a lot better. As far as I can now judge, any difficulties I encountered were certainly not due to overt resentment on the part of my classmates. Life was everywhere treacherous, however, and the Head Girlship taught me that even the good opinion of trusted adults could turn the ground under one's feet into quicksand.

My brother attended St George's, a Roman Catholic school in Kingston run by embattled Jesuits. Although John never made any close friends at the school, at least none he saw after school hours, he soon surrounded himself with schoolyard pals and seemed very much at home there, picking up a boisterous, full Jamaican schoolboy patois he alternated with our house English as needed. He seemed totally happy and generally ran with a scrawny pack of campus kids from the Mona neighborhood where we lived. Years later, it transpired he had friends in the shanty town that verged on our neighborhood, with whom he would play soccer and sometimes cricket. His best mate in this group was a young Rastafarian called Headley. John and Headley would sit chewing the fat kerb-side, waiting for brawls to break out so that Headley could jump in with his knife.

St George's occupied the greater part of John's life during term time. The school was run by one Father Quinlan, a kind old man who insisted on getting to know every single boy in the school. To this end, he would hold a brief interview with each pupil at least once a year. When my brother's turn came around – he was fourteen at the time – a curious conversation took place between them.

'Well, John, I see that your family are not Catholics,' began Father Quinlan, looking at his file.

'That's right, father, they're Church of England.'

'Hmm,' said Father Quinlan thoughtfully. 'And I see that you've never been baptized. Is that so?'

'Yes, father,' came my brother's cautious reply.

'Well, how about it then?' inquired the old Irishman in conspiratorial tones. 'What do you think?'

'I'd rather not, Father Quinlan,' said John as diplomatically as he could. 'I don't feel ready.'

'Well, I suppose you'd better not then,' conceded the headmaster. 'You're probably in a state of grace already.'

My gawky kid brother with his eternally scraped knees being 'in a state of grace' got him teased for days, but at the same time I was trying to figure out whether the priest had turned his back on that particular lamb in his young flock. Accustomed to the strictly laid down rules of some of the religious groups of my childhood, I marveled that the conceptual colors sharply delineated in the past were beginning to blend together. The elders of the tribe were openly dissolving in their appointed roles. What I had taken as facts were fading and recombining their hues on a daily basis, in a vat of multicolored dyes not all of whose tones seemed to serve either for practical purposes or for ornament.

When my father fell deathly ill – the one single fact that has forever darkened my memories of Jamaica – my faith in a beneficent Almighty was already seriously undermined. A certain boyfriend of mine, a rather sophisticated campus kid who had spent a year or two at college in Bloomington, Indiana, and was a devotee of Bob Dylan and all things that hung loose, had been trying to get me into the sack. His method consisted of demolishing all my arguments as to the existence of God as medieval superstition; at the same time, he was attempting to fill in the resulting void with a liberating philosophy of life that would right all wrongs, mainly centered around the uselessness – from a Marxist point of view – of my virginity. He showed me his outstretched palm. 'Why is it all right to touch a person *here...*' he would ask, pointing to the top of his bony thumb, 'but not *here*?' indicating a spot an inch below his pinkie. Instead of caving in, I felt betrayed and manipulated. I wept furious tears for days and sent Christopher a heartbroken, but incensed little note accusing him of disregarding a person's dignity and so obliging them to break up with the person they loved. Christopher sent me back a perfectly wrought poem in free verse, the first modern poetry I had ever seen. It described my general misery all too well, down to my grape-like eyes bloated with tears (drawn from imagination, as I had not cried in front of him), and was clearly the work of a lyric genius. It was a mere chronicle, however, showing no regret at all, so I rather redundantly cut him loose. If I had survived losing my first boyfriend, I could certainly get over this creep. Christopher Oliveira had succeeded in one thing, though. His atheistic arguments stuck. I now knew there was no God.

That same month, my mother received a devastating phone call. She was told point-blank and with no previous preparation – the doctor on the other end of the line having assumed she was expecting the news – that my father was dangerously ill and they were sending an ambulance for him that very minute. He had been spitting blood, and it was not known then whether it was cancer or tuberculosis. As my mother hung up the phone, trembling like a leaf, my father's car rushed up the driveway and stopped uncharacteristically in front of the veranda. He had arrived one minute too late to warn my mother. My mother burst into tears. 'Leave the house, Carys,' she said. 'Go out for a walk!' The last thing I saw as I left the house for the loneliest walk of my life was my parents clutched in each other's arms.

Fortunately, my father's illness turned out to be tuberculosis, not cancer, and was therefore curable. He was moved to a sanatorium in the hills for treatment. My mother threw a party to celebrate – she was the only woman, she joked, who had ever thrown a party upon learning that her husband had TB. Our misery was nevertheless deeply felt. I turned instinctively to prayer, begging the Almighty to spare my father's life, then slapping my own face in a frenzy of furious desperation as I remembered he didn't exist. It was an awful time for us all, especially perhaps my brother. As we children were not allowed to go and visit my father, John's imagination ran wild. In his mind, he pictured him in the same state as Humphrey, our white Labrador, whose ear had been bitten through in a fight and become infested with maggots. It was only after my mother took John to see a doctor – his anxiety had become overwhelming – that we were allowed to go and see my father in the hospital. He looked absolutely wonderful – pink and cheerful – and had been looking forward to our letters. John recovered very soon after, and our father was sent home after three months with instructions to swallow entire handfuls of monstrous pills several times a day.

Another circumstance writ bold on the scroll of memory is the fact I was struggling not to mind being eighteen in the fifth form and nearly twenty-one when I finally left the school. Held back yet again for coming from somewhere else, I defended my dignity and sanity – the alternative was the abyss, which could not be recognized to exist – by pretending to the world and myself I was not humiliated by still being a schoolgirl, not shamed by wearing a school uniform and bearing the certain mark of a schoolgirl – the whiteness of the feet and ankles where my uniform socks and shoes had been. A curious romantic relationship with a physician friend of my parents had been warped on both sides by the child/woman mutant imago that I, smiling cooperatively, had willed myself to be. This dear friend had managed to communicate to my parents something of his feelings for me, but was perennially awkward about saying anything directly to me because he sensed I should be involved with young men my own age – meaning my own *stage* – not with established, uncool folks like him. Tony's manner was usually bristly, occasionally interspersed with an odd, brusque joke to scratch the surface of an affectionate comment. In this vein, I received a series of veiled overtures, advances and retreats, none of which I felt I could do much about. I had worked too hard, for one thing, on my lifeboat schoolgirl persona and secondly I realized that, in deference to my parents, it would be better not to get into a socially volatile situation with one of their peers. For their part, they were respectful and discreet. They did nothing to interfere with the natural course of things, even on one occasion allowing me for the sake of convenience and logistics to travel with Tony to his place in Ocho Rios half a day ahead of the rest of the family. I was carsick on the winding way up, and we had to stop. I was embarrassed to be suffering from such a childish disorder, but Tony was, after all, a doctor. His reaction was typical of his conversations with me.

The author (on the left) with her brother and a friend at Tony's place in Ocho Rios in 1968.

'Did you take any motion-sickness tablets?' he asked in a kind of brisk growl. 'If not, why not?'

When I explained I hadn't known the road would be so rough, he softened and gave me some gentle practical advice that involved walking along the road in the fresh air. He stopped the car at a film-noir-type bar in the country run by a kind, hardbitten woman with a cigarette hanging from her lip – an ex-cop from the Bronx who was raising a dozen wild local orphans in an old double-decker London bus in her yard. She seemed to know Tony well, appeared fond of him and was very nice to me. We got into a conversation about life in general, but I had the distinct feeling she was being very diplomatic.

After his death a few years later – under suspicious circumstances in the lovely, rambling bungalow he had bought for his new career move to the north of the island – I often wondered what had been in his heart, what checks and balances he had invoked in his decision to leave his teaching and heart-wrenching practice with the malnourished children of Kingston to go and treat the gonorrhea of unruffled millionaires on the north coast of the island. I remember how, drained after long hours attending to sick and savaged children, he would arrive at our house at the same time every evening, his long American car nosing its tired way down our driveway to park by the kitchen. I would fix him his gin and tonic in silence, knowing he would be unable to speak for a good half hour.

What had I meant to Tony? Today I am certain that, if circumstances had allowed me to be a normal twenty-year-old (whatever that means), I would have known soon enough. But my self existed only as a specter of dispossession: my artificially protracted girlhood was all I could then inhabit.

It was a few years later, in a class on creoles and pidgins, that I came to know the historical background to the Jamaican patois that was spoken all over the island. Like all patois, it was a blend of a colonizing, usually European language and a 'native', often African one. In the Caribbean, the African substrate provided the rhythms and some of the syntactical structures while the European language contributed most of the vocabulary. I learned also that Jamaican patois was not merely a substandard dialect of English that had evolved out of the island's slave past, but a complex grammatical system it was possible to outrage. Although I learned to understand it well enough, it was out of the question sociologically for me to adopt it as it was very much the language of the disenfranchised, not a Jamaican mirror of my own middle-class English. Nor did I want to adopt it: it sounded overly quaint to my ear, like a soundtrack from a forties' happy-darky movie, and no part of it spoke to any need within me. What could have possibly driven me to want to absorb and foster the wretchedness with which that beautiful, lilting creole was so closely linked? That language seemed to represent the island's failure to meld its myths and realities into a functioning entity in which people could deal with each other in a humane, dignified manner. Not that the language wasn't dignified. Of itself it was. What caused me to reject it as one of my own was the pain of those who spoke it, the shabbiness with which history had treated them. I needed a deeply rooted tongue, one that would resist all impeachments of its past and future, one that would hold out to my precarious sense of self a steady hand and lay down on solid ground the strong, bright new tiles that would replace the fading foundations of my Malaysian past. The shattered wreck of Jamaica's collision of cultural intentions was not quite what I needed at that point. I walked, therefore, slightly above that debris, as pontianaks are said by Malays to walk slightly above ground level.

 Meanwhile, my formal education progressed along the lines

operating in Britain, and application to a British university was becoming a reality – one of the reasons my parents had decided to leave Malaysia. The languages offered at St Hugh's when I arrived were French and Spanish, neither of which I had ever studied. My academic situation was rather grim: I would join form five and in one year (as opposed to the normal five-year curriculum) have to prepare for the O levels. A successful outcome would then allow me to join the sixth form, where for two years I would prepare for the A levels in three subjects and on the strength of those results be accepted or not into a university. The curriculum was very different from that operating in Malaysia. Here I faced – among other subjects – Caribbean as well as European History, a hard science (Biology), some rather stiff Mathematics, Drawing (for which I possessed a liking, but no formal techniques and no particular talent) and, of course, a new language. Mrs Carnegie, the headmistress, had suggested Spanish on the grounds it was said to be easier at elementary and intermediate level than French and a student having to learn a five-year curriculum in one year might be more comfortable with it.

Spanish set my soul afire. Every cell in my brain resonated to its vivacity, its unabashedly cruel wit, the fact one went for broke and burned one's bridges in pronouncing its five rotund syllables. Yet one could also mince one's words, choosing among a rich array of diminutive and augmentative suffixes with which to hint at things one didn't quite want to say outright. Unlike the rigidity of English word order, the structure of Spanish sentences could be shuffled around to emphasize any part of the sentence one wanted, and the subjunctive mood could be elegantly deployed to show that situations were true or false maybe, possibly, doubtfully, hopefully. Staying behind after school for extra sessions with my teacher, I hungrily wolfed down vocabulary lists, verb tenses, idioms. I devoured books listing proverbs and jokes. I sought out Spanish speakers wherever I could. I acquired pen pals from Colombia, Uruguay and Spain, and wrote to them avidly. I read books by Blasco Ibáñez and Pérez Galdós as well as Gerald Brenan's *The Spanish Labyrinth* and George Orwell's *Homage to Catalonia*. I was transfixed – although I later came to repudiate it – by Hemingway's *For Whom the Bell Tolls*. I would capture a brave reality through the Spanish tongue, infuse myself with its noble past, its present audacity, its sense of having hit the world's nails uncompromisingly on the head. I longed to visit Al-Andalus, Tordesillas, León, the Alpujarra, the Spanish Pyrenees. Nor was my infatuation limited to the Iberian Peninsula. My daydreams were filled with South American names such as Patagonia, Sucre, Cochabamba and others like Quetzalcoatl and Popocatépetl I was convinced I would never learn to pronounce, but whose enthralling written shapes I acknowledged like those of thrillingly enigmatic characters in an overpopulated Russian novel.

School life was reasonably happy, and I made several good friends. My closest pal was a smiling, excitable girl called Cheryl Hawkins with whom I would spend lazy weekends – often linked to a party we were planning to attend – at each other's houses, talking endlessly about boyfriends and consulting each other over homework problems. The Hawkinses were from the Turks Islands, and her grandmother would make Turks dishes for us and scare us with surrealistic stories about zombie cows with gold teeth. One year, I decided to throw a party for my birthday, and Cheryl and I worked out all the details together with my mother. I invited several good friends from our class, a number of boys I knew from various events, including a decent contingent of upperclassmen from St George's, my brother's school, and a small handful of young folks from the neighborhood. Tony

Daniels was also invited and was going to help dish out the punch. We calculated finger food for about twenty-five.

There was a girl in class who had turned her face against me since the day I joined the school. I had had no trouble making friends with other girls from the science stream, but Christine Hillier always went out of her way to exclude me from any conversations and often turned her back when I addressed her, as if I were not in the room at all. I tried as hard as I could to figure out what I had done to annoy her, but with no luck. After a while, I talked it over with Cheryl, who told me that Christine was probably jealous of the fact I was from Europe and so must think myself a cut above her. It didn't help, Cheryl added, that Christine knew I had an active social life beyond school. This was puzzling. Christine was a bright student who ran with a clannish, high-flying crowd that frequented hotel discos en masse on weekends. She seemed to be at the very top of the social food chain, or at least the chain we knew. Anyway, I decided to invite her to the party as a sign of good faith, thinking we could get to know each other a little better and things would sort themselves out between us.

The invitation itself was quite an ordeal. I spent a long time at school trying to track her down when she was alone and, when I finally hailed her outside the assembly hall, she looked at me as if I had just crawled out of a drain.

'Hey, Christine, I was just thinking. I'm having a party next Saturday and I was wondering if you'd like to come. We never did get much of a chance to get together and I thought it might be fun.'

Her face brightened somewhat, then darkened again. 'Who's going?' she asked, suddenly haughty, lifting up her nose so she could look down it at me.

'Well, you know,' I stammered, shocked at the question.

'Some girls from class and some friends of mine from home. And then there'll be a bunch of guys from St George's.'

This brought no response apart from a fierce sniff. I tried harder. I knew the St George's boys would be a star attraction, so I added lamely, 'It'll be fun to see what they're wearing and how they carry on.'

I knew this was a dumb thing to say, but Christine was a gorgon and I was no match for her. She could turn me into a quivering idiot at the drop of a hat, and I was floundering.

'Where do you live?' she asked brusquely.

When Christine turned up to the party, she brought a retinue of about forty people with her, most of whom I had never seen in my life and none of whom ever bothered to come over to say hello to me or my mother. At first, I gadded about, trying to welcome every new face personally, but after a while I gave up because most of them stared back at me in vague puzzlement. The group had swarmed into the house through the open French doors, paid no attention to anyone else at the party and helped themselves so copiously and autonomously to hors d'oeuvres and punch that Tony had literally to stand guard at my parents' bar to keep them off the bottles of the real hard stuff. When supplies ran out – the gatecrashers had arrived somewhat late in any case – they asked in loud, sneering voices why there was no drink at this stinking party. A few couples turned out the light in my father's study – right next to the living room – and took possession of the divan there. After about fifteen minutes, my mother turned the light back on and winkled them politely but firmly out.

In spite of all this, which we later learned was standard procedure in certain urban teenage circles, people seemed to be having a good time, and we thought the party had been a success. School life resumed. Before the week was out, however, I began to realize several girls were glaring strangely at me and some wouldn't even speak to me. Nobody would tell me what the matter was. By Friday evening I had been snubbed so often and by so many people I thought were friends that I was a nervous wreck. I turned to Cheryl, who had herself been acting a little peculiarly.

'I don't understand it,' I said. 'People are being horrible to me, even Suzanne and Lizzie.'

To my surprise, Cheryl burst immediately into repressed tears. 'I know,' she gasped. 'I'm so sorry, Carys. I didn't want to tell you, but, since it's all come out, they've been saying such terrible things about you!'

'What are they saying?' I asked, my heart contracted to the size of a pea.

'That, when you asked Christine to the party, you said, "And there'll be a lot of black boys there. It'll be fun to see what they wear and how they carry on!"'

I sat down in a chair, hands over my eyes, absolutely overwhelmed. 'That's not what I said!' I stammered. 'That's not at all what I said!'

In the conversation that followed, I repeated to Cheryl exactly what had been said when I invited Christine to the party. I asked Cheryl to recount exactly who she had heard the story from. It had been repeated by quite a number of our good friends. What really stunned me was not that Christine had chosen to spread such a malicious lie around – she was obviously sick and twisted – but that decent people had believed it. People who knew better. People who knew me well.

I took the rest of the day off from school, feigning illness, and cried for hours in my bedroom. There was no way I thought I would ever get over this betrayal. This was a perverted society, rotten to the core. I couldn't wait to get out.

My mother thought I should inform the headmistress of Christine's smear campaign, so that the wrong could be righted, but I was just too upset by the whole affair even to consider digging into that foul mud any further. What would be the use? The girls had never seen any signs of racism in me all the time I had been at St Hugh's, they knew very well there was no way I could ever have said what had been attributed to me, but they had been quick to seize the opportunity to 'believe' the story nevertheless. Either they believed it or they did not, and in either case they had acted according to some deep inner impulses to which facts were irrelevant, for nobody had thought to investigate what had really happened.

I tried to struggle on as if nothing had occurred, and some of the girls who had been traitors began to smile at me again and include me in the general social to and fro of class. But I despised them. If they'd counted me a friend, why had they turned against me? Was it that they had never trusted me in the first place and Christine's story had merely ratified their fears? The pain was indelible, not least because I had felt in my own flesh that truth and justice do not always win out in the end.

I dug my heels into my work and did well enough in the exams to be admitted to the sixth form with its A-level courses. To my joy, I had swung things well enough in Spanish to be allowed to select that subject, together with English Literature and History, as a specialty. It was assumed I would go on to read English at university. That idea did not sit too well with me. Feverishly I began to apply to different branches of Her Majesty's Armed Forces, and my father kindly typed up all the letters.

The time for my admission to college coincided with my father's return to England; his three-year tour in Jamaica had been part of a five-year contract as a senior lecturer at York University. Life in Britain was a daunting prospect – what would

I have in common with my peers? Identifying with England's Glorious Literature and knowing all about Guy Fawkes Day and Nancy Mitford was clearly not going to be enough. I needed some solid ground and so applied to York University's language program, where I could specialize in Spanish linguistics and choose an 'exotic' new language from among Mandarin, Hindi, Swahili, Russian and Arabic. I would also (oh, bliss!) spend my second year in obligatory study at Seville. By the time I returned, I thought, I would be ready to face anything on my own, even life in England after my parents' next move. I had decided not to follow in my father's footsteps and read English as I calculated that one year under my parents' tutelage would be sufficient to get me on my way and, despite my qualms about England, being a student in the same department would be overly claustrophobic. With the allure of Spanish and Seville in mind, I signed on to do a main in linguistics, specializing in Spanish, and a subsidiary in philosophy.

I was shocked to discover on the first day of term that in a curious oversight my father had omitted to inform me he would be employed in his capacity as a semanticist and therefore teach in both the language and the philosophy departments. The departmental schedule underwent some deep revisions to avoid our ever having to come into academic contact, and many students never made the connection between the scholarly Ellis Evans and my good self, but I suspect some of the faculty secretly expected more of me than they were ever to receive. Be that as it may, York University provided me with my first enthralling taste of academic voyeurism, the thrill of being officially allowed to decipher what was going on in people's heads when they spoke. Disdaining Noam Chomsky as an academic circus barker with one or two good practical ideas, I learned as little about descriptive linguistics as I could possibly get away with, concentrating instead on sociological and anthropological linguistics – the real effects of language upon real people. At the same time, the phonetics and history of the Spanish language, of which I was by now totally enamored, provided me with a multi-layered, diachronic view of Spanish speech. These were concrete matters I could devote myself to. The shifting sands of my coming of age would be solid rock once more as I walked firmly forward to the words of Antonio Machado's beautiful poem:

Caminante, no hay camino,
se hace camino al andar.
Al andar se hace camino,
y al volver la vista atrás
se ve la senda que nunca
se ha de volver a pisar.

The author with friends during her year abroad in Seville.

3 SPANISH EYES

I arrived in Seville, gasping for new air. It was the fall of 1970, and I had just spent a year at York University in the most abject social misery. Most of the students there at the time were hell-bent on being 'students', which in the Britain of the time was a very specific thing. You were generally of a certain age (it was very difficult for non-traditional students, known as 'mature' students, to find the money to go to university once they had missed the first boat, when one got a grant from the government). People always went to a university far from their home towns so that, quarantined from the anti-academic undertow of home life, they would be free to pick up and act upon any new ideas on life that had come their way in the course of an education. A student was by no means just a person who happened to be going to university: he or she was an entity unanchored by parental or other conventional mores, bound to be bedraggled and probably filthy in his or her personal habits, not fit to rent a house. Students were mostly poverty-stricken because the grants we received from the government had been issued overly optimistically on the basis of a means test applied to our parents. One young man I knew whose parents were castle-owning aristocrats was almost constantly famished: the government considered them too wealthy for their child to be awarded a grant, but they themselves had no actual cash. They also believed the boy had no business running off to read philosophy: he should be at home learning to run the estate. Nobody seemed to have any taste for conversation – at least not the freshmen – a wretched state of affairs for one whose life until then had transpired in a busy thicket of conversation.

People were very much aware of having been handpicked from the top percentile of the nation's youth and therefore officially not just anybody. To some, this was heady stuff, almost as heady as the new identity people were acquiring as they passed around their de rigueur joints smoked rather self-consciously in groups like peace pipes. I believe, if I had been raised in Britain, I would have made more friends: I would have known who Pink Floyd was, for example, or what the Who had just put out. Nobody wanted to hear about Malaysia in the least. Nor did anyone seem to be caught up in the fierce revolutionary zeal that had overrun French and German universities in 1968 and begun the slow, but inexorable move away from the dinosaur enclosure constituted by a number of academic and social institutions. The people I knew just wanted to look beautiful in their own dishevelment, to assume vast, beatific wisdom based on other people's trips to ashrams and to embrace whatever it was their parents couldn't understand. To all extents and purposes, I was one of the parents. I had come willing to examine the land of my birth culture, but cringed at the thought of the psychedelia that was swirling around the residence halls, stealing the desire to converse from people's mouths, forcing people to follow its own guidelines as they formed groovy personalities. Worst of all, I couldn't believe how much they all wanted to be exactly the same, embracing only the foreignness that had received the imprimatur of rock stars. I made some good friends within the language department, but beyond that I would inevitably gravitate to foreign graduate students, who – perhaps because they had already broken out of their home molds – were more worldly and tended to be interested in conversation for its own sake.

The fact that during my first year I lived at home did not help my inner isolation. I was devastatingly lonely – a Malaysian girl strained through the accidental colander of Jamaica. My compatriots were as different from me as they possibly could be, and I didn't want to be like them in the least. But few people knew I was a Malaysian in a Brit's skin and needed help in getting to know the culture. It was assumed I knew the culture, was saturated with it to the point of nausea and all I should want to do was to slough it off by tuning in and dropping out. It seemed to me there was nothing to admire in my nation and, although I had met some wonderful people, I would generally come home in the evening for dinner and stay in, never really forming a cohesive group of my own. I made my own clothes to my own idea of individuality and purpose – rather eccentric ones such as an ankle-length skirt made out of a wooly blanket against the bitter York winds, sheath-like items in golden orange, reminiscent of a cheongsam, and a gaudy gypsy affair in multicolored, striped satin. I had never owned a pair of jeans in my life – they were the one sartorial item my father had forbidden as we grew up – and I was not about to start now. Somehow I survived my first year at York. I left for

Seville with the hope that, by the grace of God, I would be able to bear England a little better during the two years left after my return.

Seville was exactly what I wanted: a storied city redolent of its Arabic past and exploding with vital spirit. I fell in love with absolutely everything I saw: the mysterious, pulsing Jewish quarter with its gentle fountains and family houses built around inner courtyards planted with bright flowers and orange trees; the Moorish alcazar, its palace of luxurious staterooms a flask in which the luminous intellect of the Moors would be preserved intact, their clear, aesthetic vision made even sharper by the fact the rooms, stripped of furniture and therefore pre-empting thoughts of creature comforts, were lined by geometric blue and white tiles so as not to offend Allah with the representation of mankind. I heard many legends of wise and loving Moorish kings, like the caliph in Granada who planted for his homesick Christian queen a sweep of almond trees across the sierra so that, when the trees blossomed in the spring, they would resemble the snow-swept mountains of her homeland. I loved the gypsy Triana quarter, where the best exponents of *cante hondo* and the sultriest dancers of flamenco cried or stamped out their tortured art exposed only in small gatherings. I loved the grandiose, historic buildings that served the administration of the New World. I loved the Seville idiom, rapier-witty as a matter of course and glittering in the bright sun. I loved the elegance and courtesy of the people I met, the dignity of children, like solemn little men and women, the instant hospitality of the homes where I was welcomed. I loved the daily bar scene with its sharp, evocative sherries, the tapas impregnated with the same flair, it seemed to me, as the dashing, slightly lisping language and the attitude that life was devil-may-care. I loved the religious processions of Easter week, each with floats of the Virgin Mary or a Christ either crucified or on the road to crucifixion, borne on the backs of faithful brotherhoods, accompanied by penitents and ablaze with the light of a thousand moving candles. I loved my classes at the university, which was full of the scent of Spain's Golden Age. Franco's regime was in full swing. I didn't notice, I didn't care. I loved it all and bought the package as advertised. This was not England: this was a place of purpose, where people were smartly groomed and self-aware, applauded the ballet of the bullfight and knew the value of élan and wit. I lived for a year in this sharply delineated poster whose uncompromising glamour no contradictory aesthetic could dislodge.

I made sure to fall in love with the first reasonably presentable man that came my way and in the vulnerability of my nakedness – for I had had my Malaysian vestments ripped away and the heavy English ones had never fit – eagerly undertook the role of the Andalusian *novia* of the time. It was something to be. I learned a vast amount of colloquial Spanish through this delimited, adopted persona, was presented to many fascinating and a great number of anodyne people. I was repressed in many ways, discouraged from writing, asked not to laugh too loud, but felt I was learning to belong and my embarrassing, rough edges would be filed away sufficiently for me to belong fully one day. My language would match the identity I had embraced. I would be witty too, but virtuously so.

So when Roberto wrote to call it all off in my final year at York, where I had returned to finish up the two remaining years of my degree before returning definitively to Seville, I lost everything. The devastation of that final rejection was made all the more cruel by the fact I had lost the identity I had built so assiduously. I was truly nothing.

I fell into a smothered despair, unable to leave Alcuin College, my residence hall, much less ride on public transport, and unable to tell my friends what had happened. I knew that, solid as they were in their home-grown identities, they would never be able to understand how hard it would be for me survive this; I believed that, in their kind, but comfortable way, they could never fathom beyond the usual heartbreaking depths of loss of love.

Nevertheless, even through this traumatic period, I was convinced that Spain was to be the backdrop of my destiny and its language, so consonant with my spirit, could be claimed forever. One day, I stopped weeping just long enough to hear about an opportunity for linguistic research in Spain for British graduates. I applied and was awarded a grant by the Spanish government to study the loss of a certain preposition in internominal position. I chose to do so in Salamanca, the home of the most famous university in the land and a universe away from the charms of Andalusia. I prayed that survival would eventually dawn over the desert of my life, drawn by the clanking, inexorable carriage of research into linguistic evolution.

Salamanca served as an emotional no man's land I traversed in an hypnotic state, dead but for an eviscerating hurt and a desire to hear my emptiness expressed. I saw, learned and wrote, wandered about the fabled golden sandstone of the city's storied monuments and moved familiarly in the bars and cafés around its stunning Plaza Mayor. I was getting somewhere and had many friends I loved. However, I saw and felt everything as if through a gray fog. When my student visa was about to run out and I was doomed to return to foreign olde England, I received the most astonishing stroke of good luck. A friend told me a certain professor of English was about to take up a chair in Santiago de Compostela and was looking for a second assistant to go with him. A meeting was immediately arranged for me with Dr Cardeñosa in the lounge of a well-known downtown hotel.

As I perched on the edge of an expensively brocaded, painfully shaped faux medieval chair, Dr Cardeñosa fixed his large, orange-flecked eyes on my face and spoke to me gently and clearly about how things would be for me at the University of Santiago. To his great credit, he never let fall the slightest hint of his concern as to whether I could be trusted to support him in a job which, I later discovered, promised to be the slightest bit difficult for him politically. He began his description with a gambit that sounded vaguely like aversion therapy. The area, I was told, was possessed of great natural beauty – the beaches were among Spain's most breathtaking – but the place was inaccessible and underdeveloped; few roads led in and out of Galicia, and so one could easily feel isolated there. In addition, Galicians were reserved and suspicious, taking years to trust outsiders enough to forge real friendships. On the upside, however, it seemed they were very much easier to teach than Castilians because, being bilingual already and by dint of having been historically exposed as sailors and émigrés to the outside world, they were not fazed by foreign languages. My job would be to provide practical support for students already learning English grammar, literature and history of the language, as well as Middle English and some basic notions of Anglo-Saxon. All these subjects would be taught by specialists. I would administer and teach five full days a week of English conversation. My prospects sounded excellent, but here Dr Cardeñosa stopped to look at me even more firmly, as if to make sure I wasn't going to bolt. The position, he continued carefully, was described as a *lectorado de inglés*, or readership in English, and would unfortunately only last a year, at the end of which I would resign the job in favor of the British graduate student for whom the post had already been reserved. I would be paid an exiguous stipend each month (here Dr Cardeñosa mentioned a sum that would keep me just this side short of homelessness) and, since the job could never be wholly legal despite its existing under the auspices of a respected government body (there was no such category as *lectora* contemplated by Spanish law), I would receive no health or other benefits. It would also be necessary to leave the country every six months in order to get my passport stamped as a tourist, for that is what I would officially be.

I informed Dr Cardeñosa I was very interested in the position and was hired on the spot. I skipped out of the café's heavy portals into a Plaza Mayor that suddenly looked clear and well defined. I was delirious with joy. A job in Spain! In Santiago de Compostela! At a university! For a whole year!

No sooner had the news spread among my Castilian friends that I had landed a post in Santiago de Compostela in the nation's misty northwest than I was deluged with pieces of lore that were as astounding as they were contradictory. Galicia, it seemed, occupied a disquieting patch of psychological territory marked 'Here Be Dragons' by the rest of Spain while at the same time serving as a mystical catch-all, a place that induced people to go off on little recitals that invariably ran along the lines of 'Ay, Santiago is the resting place of St James, the spiritual fount of our nation, a balsam for the soul of Spain!' followed by a baffled and slightly envious comment on the sexual freedom of the *galega*. Then there were the witches-and-spooks snippets of information imparted in knowing, somewhat patronizing tones barded lavishly with the schmaltz of the last-minute airport souvenir. An ingredient always present in these contradictory salads was a sort of recipe kit for a Pan-Celtic Twilight, complete with tales of bagpipes and whirling jigs. The brightest colors of all, however, the ones that caused people to wax the most spirited, were splashed all over the gaudy, anecdote-filled palette used to describe the brutal backwardness of the area's country people. I was presented with everything the Castilian thought about the *galego*. Above all, I would be solemnly anointed with a blessing in the form of a warning: 'Watch your heart! The *gallegas* are so beguiling, their speech so honeyed, no foreign man ever leaves Galicia without a wife!' It was clear this was ritual advice always given to males departing for Galicia, but in my case people would tag on a formula more suited to my gender: 'So you'll have lots of competition up there!' or even, kindly though somewhat distractedly, 'But you'll do okay, you're very sweet too!'

An aspect of being Galician that invariably seemed to exasperate outsiders was an apparent habit of answering a question with another question. The following scenario was enacted for me in numerous Salamanca cafés, most memorably by Mario, an ex-seminarian friend from Córdoba then studying philosophy at the Pontifical University. We were sitting in the Plaza Mayor, finishing a cup of coffee, when I broke the news that I was off to Santiago.

'Well, it's true, Mario,' I said, 'I got the job! I'm leaving in September!'

'Mother of God, Carys!' he gasped, reaching to grab me as if he expected me to jump up and fly out the window to catch the very next northbound train. 'By the nails of the crucifixion of Christ, don't get mixed up with those Galicians!'

'Why ever not, Mario?' I grinned, digging in my purse for money to pay a hovering waiter.

'Because!'

'Because why?'

'They're just loathsome and twisted, not straight-up folks like us!' replied Mario at last, assuming a reasoned, well-thinking expression. Jumping to his feet, he bent over, circling a fist in imitation of a motorist rolling down a car window. Neck politely craned, he innocently made as if to address an invisible Galician peasant apparently standing off to one side, 'Good afternoon, sir. Is it far to the town hall?'

Mario then morphs into a suspicious, canny peasant, who counters, 'Why do you ask?'

At this, Mario affects an all-consuming fury. Thumping the table, he sits down harshly in his chair, flinging ragged peanut husks from an unstable saucer in all directions as he does so. 'Can you believe it? What a jerk! Why can't he just say yes or no? What kind of perverse mind must a man have to answer a straightforward question in that antisocial way! The trouble with those backward sons of whores is that they can't wait to be unhelpful to strangers. I shit on their mothers!'

Mario paused for a moment, only to come back with one last outburst, 'Be careful, Carys, be careful! When you say hello to one of those bastards on a stairway, you can never figure out whether they're going up or down!'

The Galicians, it appeared, were mysterious people who drank brutishly, barked like dogs at the most innocent of questions and lived in damp, nebulous realms of ignorance above their own stinking cowsheds. Sometimes I would receive this line of information in the very same breath as the news that the *galego* was a generous, hardworking northern soul infused with *morriña* – a kind of creeping, soul-rotting homesickness the Portuguese call *saudade* and the Welsh *hiraeth* – which works upon him like a slow death when he is separated from his homeland. And yet, as I had heard, there were the haunting poems of Rosalía de Castro, the hair-raising, naturalistic stories of Emilia Pardo Bazán, considered such a virago in her time, and the terrifying dramatic and lyric genius of Ramón del Valle-Inclán. But these were figures no one in Castile mentioned in my café-society crash course on Galicia.

Thankfully I was to become familiar with references to these authors first through the descriptions of their compatriots, then directly through their works themselves, along with many other writers and painters of that lush, gentle land. In the meantime, I waited impatiently for the day to come for me to fly to the richly nuanced contradictions of Santiago and away from the beautiful, lofty, but uncompromisingly cut and dried world of Castile and its glorious past.

Perhaps I was too primed with tales of the Galician supernatural to think of Santiago de Compostela in guidebook terms, but, when I first arrived, I immediately sensed I'd come home. There was no overwhelming desire to go tramping the streets of the old city, sucking everything in, or to wallow in that massive river of blurred beauty. I merely felt a soothing welcome as if I were in fact already a part of the place, not a transient about to be changed forever.

The historic part of the town included a bustling, wine-stained warren of narrow streets lined with bars and restaurants, each one crammed with students. Some of these streets would lead unexpectedly to the magnificent buildings that bear witness to the founding institutions of this center of pilgrimage: convents, seminaries, canonical buildings, smaller churches, noble houses, museums. The busiest streets of all led straight to the stunning Obradoiro Square, bounded on all four sides by the twelfth-century Romanesque cathedral, the impressive Hostelry of the Catholic Monarchs Ferdinand and Isabella, the town hall and the ancient university administrative building. Students pullulated absolutely everywhere, day and night. From my house in Fonseca Square, shared with several fellow novice members of my department, I could hear their Welsh-sounding Galician drinking songs far into the wee hours. Soon I had convivial friends of my own, and in no time at all it seemed

I had never not been one of those voices, singing those same lilting shanties, raunchy parodies and, as the night wore on, heart-rending laments.

This language sounded notes within me that may have been a mere wishful dream of my parents' homeland, a place where words burst with the longings of people's hearts. It flowed gently and sweetly to my newcomer's ear, its rhythms affectionate, almost coaxing. Speech was formed of soft diphthongs, words charmingly ended in -*de* and curious little grammatical shortcuts. Words steeped their referents in a flavor that was at once medieval and intensely fresh. And, as befits a matriarchal land, the men's intonations were as fluid as the women's. This was a singing world that called to key notes in the well spring of my spirit. I knew that, to answer in its own cadence, I must first allow my heart to open outward. But I was nowhere near ready.

Instead, I would perfect my Spanish, a clear, transparent tongue spoken here in accents and rhythms far different from those of my entrapment. I would master Castilian, infuse it with reality and, once I had bent it to my will, grab hold of life once more through its clear-eyed flexibility.

The city came to my aid. The Praza da Quintana, also known as the Quintana dos Mortos, soon imprinted me with my own interpretation of what a country's spiritual fount could be. Built at a beautifully sculpted side exit to the cathedral and on a much frequented route between the bars of the high part of the old city and the impressive Obradoiro, the Quintana had always remained miraculously and serenely immune from the general hubbub. The square was built over a burial ground, the fourth-century site of worship of the followers of the moon-bathing, heretical priest Priscillian, the *mortos* of its name long forgotten under the flagstones. But, long before I discovered this, I often felt the presence of layers upon layers of prayer accumulated over the intervening centuries by generations of nuns in reclusion at the monastery whose high wall formed one side of the square. One could almost hear the masses sung or mumbled by priests and the hushed responses of pilgrims ancient and modern at the cathedral's many altars and sense the townspeople's secret longings configured, recognized and set free in this granite nexus between worlds. For the pilgrims who have been flocking to Santiago for centuries, it is clearly the cathedral, the seat of ancient welcoming traditions and the long awaited, hard sought catharsis of confession and pardon, that forms the essence of the city, but for me it is the Quintana that encapsulates both *samsara* and nirvana: the sharing with the pilgrims of the past of their journey and its resolution. The square offered a secret sense of healing among the otherwise happy whirligig of my frantically busy life.

At some point in the eleventh century, a pope decreed that every year in which St James' Day fell on a Sunday would be a 'jubilee' year, when repentant pilgrims who had duly confessed their sins in Santiago de Compostela would receive remission in purgatory of all their previous wrongdoings. The boom in foot-travel that ensued was remarkable, and the whole Santiago pilgrim tradition was born, including the creation of favored routes from various lands, hostelries along those routes, charitable hospitals, the crafting of jet talismans to keep the travelers safe from harm and, over time, a rich pool of legends religious and secular. The Napoleonic Wars interrupted the flow of wayfarers for a while, but it soon resumed and has continued to this day. It is usually not possible to distinguish a pilgrim from a tourist since many come initially as the latter, intending to replenish their spiritual coffers while there. This group as easily pours into the city from a tour bus, a train or an airplane.

The footsore, walking pilgrims from France, Germany and England, who have often planned and looked forward to this spiritual exercise for years, are an inspiring sight with their bedrolls and water bottles. The city offers certain benefits to these sorts of pilgrim as long as they can show proof (usually a stamp from the refuges where they have stayed) that they have completed one of the designated routes from their homeland.

In literature, the foreigner is often an enigmatic, if not tragic, figure, not always because of anything he or she has done: the mystery arises from the desire in the mind of the observer as to what that person may embody beyond the reach of the pedestrian stay-at-home. Many women from more liberal parts of Europe (and what parts were not more liberal than Franco's Spain?) have commented on the fact that, during the sixties and seventies, light-haired females were marked as walking, single-member brothels. Certain movies were partly responsible for this: a laugh and a drool could always be raised by the antics of the comic Spanish peasant off to 'Europe' in search of a job and by the comedy of errors that would invariably ensue with an overly busty, nymphomaniac Swede. Adding to this view was the government-sponsored boom in cheap tourism, which brought hordes of Germans and Britons to the beaches and two weeks of a seemingly unreal bender, including the inevitable cocktail of drinking, brawling, sunning and general debauchery, not to mention the spending of money that seemed no less real. The hotels were not real, nor was any furniture they demolished, nor any local noses they punched. Their behavior wasn't real either: everything would vanish as they boarded the plane home, having had a 'fabulous' time in sunny Spain. So a foreign woman, particularly a young one, had a lot to live down and a lot to fight off. This had been my experience in the Seville of 1970, made even more maddening by the fact I did not identify myself with the same cultural background as my hosts did.

Galicia, however, offered greater complexities, some of them worth a giggle or two. Among my colleagues at the university, there was a handful of individuals that had me pegged as a particular type of Englishwoman. Many of these cultural bingo games were played out in the Reyna Café, where lecturers and students from the Faculty of Philosophy and Letters often went for a mid-morning coffee. Here it was that one particular Latin lecturer confessed to me his love of the English Romantics and quoted swooning lines from Byron and Keats in a fairly decent translation. He looked crushed when it became clear my knowledge was nowhere near as profound as his: he had convinced himself that I was a literary scholar. Equally disappointing were my exotic tales of a tropical past: he would much have preferred sober accounts of tea on the lawn in the vicarage garden. It took about two years for his dream to fall away, and he and his wife have remained good friends ever since. In the eyes of another friend – strangely enough, also a classicist (perhaps this has something to do with the love of mythology) – I was emblematic of heady, youthful days on London's Carnaby Street among the mini-skirted dolly birds and insouciant Volkswagens painted in bright, swirling LSD flowers, happy days when all the world was blithe and gay and visiting Spaniards could forget the dictatorship at home.

When my initial teaching year passed and I was replaced by Jeremy, the charming and talented young Englishman who had been promised the position before I arrived, I had to find an alternate way to earn my living. Fortunately, a knowledge of English was considered essential for advancement within the medical and other professions and the town was full of young physicians and other professionals eager to acquire this accomplishment. There were also many university students who wished to get a head start on their future careers by learning and practicing as much English as they could, and soon I was swamped with a very eclectic clientele and plunged into an ever widening circle of acquaintances.

During this time, a friend passed me a copy of Christopher Isherwood's *Goodbye to Berlin*, the first book I read by that author. I was intrigued by his descriptions of different elements of Berlin society at the beginning of the rise of the Third Reich and by his adventures as a language tutor for different families, where, as he comically relates, he held a position that commanded treatment on a sliding scale between that of housemaid and physician. I felt I had found a kindred spirit. I also loved the entrée into different households, the kaleidoscopic changes in ambience, the fact I always found it impossible to maintain a teaching relationship that was not also that of confidante, the abrupt change in English level and requirements from one student to the next. My finances were sometimes precarious, however, for, although I had as many classes as I could fit into the day, I was still not confident enough in my professional persona to impose certain rules and, as I had become everybody's best buddy, I felt I couldn't hold them to certain financial commitments. Clients would often cancel classes at the last minute (sometimes even on the spot) and then not pay me for them at the end of the month. When pushed for precious study hours at exam time, college students would cancel class for the rest of the academic term. Also, as money from home began to run out, the classes would tend to lose their former educational priority. Sometimes I would be hired to teach a group of a certain number and arrive to find one or two extra pupils had been added at the last minute without any consultation or adjustment in the fees. The students often assumed it was all the same to me whether I taught two or seven students at a time since I was presumably earning a proper fee for an hour's work. I once came to an agreement with one particular society matron to teach elementary English three times a week to a pair of angelic little girls of seven and eight, both true beginners. When I arrived for our first class, there was an extra child waiting for me, an insufferable boy of twelve who already had several years of English and would therefore effectively cause two separate classes to be conducted simultaneously. As it turned out, he was the true object of the class as he had been doing poorly at school and his mother had been given an ultimatum from the principal. His sisters had been deployed as bait to catch a tutor who might not have taken him on otherwise. After one excruciating session during which the manipulations of the average problem child were displayed to an embarrassing degree, I left the mother a note saying I had unexpectedly been given extra responsibilities at the university and regretting I could not teach her delightful children after all. I set them up with a redoubtable British girl who was doing her year abroad and never returned to the house again. (There was another reason for my relief: the society matron had barraged me with furtive questions about my marital status and living arrangements and continued to so do for years afterward, whenever I bumped into her in the street.)

There often lurked behind the inconsiderate behavior of certain language tutees the belief that a native speaker of any given foreign language was automatically a teacher of it, language pedagogy was as easily accomplished as breathing and I was therefore making pots of money just by being myself. Many people didn't care whether one had a degree in linguistics or had barely made it through high school, whether one's spoken English was acceptable in most circles or one sounded like the disheveled convict Magwitch in *Great Expectations*: the triumph was to say one had employed a *nativo*. Americans, no matter how well educated, were generally looked down upon as ignoramuses and were at the bottom of the ladder of *desiderati*. Irish women, particularly nuns from high-class convents, were for some arcane reason thought to speak the very best English, closely followed by persons from Oxford, whether graduates of that city's illustrious university or not. So, by sheer virtue of my linguistic background, I became a kind of Mary Poppins, flying from one house to another, umbrella and books in hand, to teach and learn. A year later, however, when I was re-employed by the university in 1976, I was able to pick and choose my clients with a more weathered eye and take fewer private classes than before.

I forged several treasured friendships in those days among my private students, notably with the courtly and sensitive Dr Rogelio González Abraldes, an eminent gastroenterologist who took classes from me twice a week to relax from his many responsibilities. He would hone his already excellent, perceptive knowledge of English by making copious, detailed notes throughout our multi-themed conversations. I still remember his fascination at the word 'lurid', which surfaced in one of our close readings of a *Newsweek* article. He immediately understood my triumphant bilingual (Castilian and Galician) definition of it as *escabroso y rechamante*. Another good friend was a garrulous, affectionate ophthalmologist taking English as a sop to his professional conscience, whose eye-opening horror stories (no pun intended) and other anecdotes from the hospital would be the main course at our thrice-weekly meetings. The most energetic classes I gave were to the Coira siblings, a diverse clutch of extremely talented, unendingly generous young folks from Lugo whose widely frequented, if unwitting, postmodern salon (if they had thought they were running a salon, they would have probably shut their doors) was to become the sounding board for some of my later literary efforts. I spent many happy weekends at their country house, one of several lines of guests of all ages, nationalities and conditions, all of whom had many good personal reasons to appreciate this family's down-to-earth and open friendship.

Thanks to these and other tutoring positions I was provided with an outsider's wondering view of English syntax and vocabulary. Whereas Rogelio might inquire as to the difference between, for example, 'ambling', 'sashaying' and 'meandering' or request an explanation of the precise contextual difference between 'shall' and 'will', one of the Coiras might start up a riotous chorus against the illogicality of the English prepositional verbs and then gleefully demand restitution as if I had personally made up the entire crazy language myself. The Coira classes would take place around a circular table, like a jolly séance. With so many brains ticking at once, I was never sure what would come up. One day, María Amparo threw up her hands over the bugbear of all Spanish students of English: prepositional verbs.

'No wonder the English are all fit to be tied!' she exclaimed. 'Just look at the verb "to put up with"!'

Here she made for 'put' the motion of placing a book down on the large, round table, followed by a raising of the book to signify 'up' and then she brought it cherishingly to her chest to represent 'with'. 'Where's the logic of that? And look – they also have "to put up", "to put in for", "to put about", "to put one over on". The list goes on and on. I give up!'

María Amparo was an excellent student, though, as was her brother José Antonio, whose compositions, much to the hilarity of the others, invariably looked like screen plays.

Sometimes a student would declare undying affection for one word or another. 'Rain' was often cited as a beautifully evocative word, probably because its very Galician diphthong somehow linked it to the gentle pervasion of the regional variety of precipitation. 'Navy blue' was once mysteriously put forward by an eight-year-old pupil as his favorite English term. This young man caused me no end of worry at the beginning of our series of classes. His parents were bosom pals of a very close friend of mine who, despite the fact that by then I did not 'do' children, had entreated me so fervently to take Xabier on I suspected some dark tragedy of feudal proportions would occur if I didn't. Xabier was a sweet enough kid, well-mannered and as attentive as anyone can be at that age, and the extra classes were intended merely to give him an extra edge at school, where he was doing well. But, as the first class progressed, I became more and more convinced he had a severe hearing problem. When asked to repeat vocabulary I would pronounce for him, Xabier would spit out imaginary words that had no resemblance whatsoever to what I had just said.

'Come on, Xabier, "fire truck",' I would start encouragingly, removing a tiny Luke Skywalker from the table to a nearby shelf.

'"Meerbody"!' would come the willing reply, and Xabier would jump up in a flash, swooping down in triumph a model of Princess Leia from the same shelf.

I became very anxious when I first heard this deviant type of repetition and knew I was in above my head. Dyslexia was not a concept many people were familiar with at the time: I certainly wasn't. I was, however, well accustomed to the perplexing phenomenon of parental refusal to acknowledge problems in their children and, to make matters worse, this particular child's father was a physician and his mother a highly engaged elementary school teacher. To suggest to these two delightful people that the scion of their house might suffer from any kind of imperfection would be tantamount to implying they had not been observing their son with the same attention they had dispensed toward the children of others.

My friend María Jesús, an elementary teacher, came to my rescue. 'Why don't you ask him to imitate the sounds different animals make?' she suggested. 'That usually clarifies matters.'

The next day I tried our vocabulary list again. '"Airplane"!' I enunciated as cheerfully and clearly as I could.

'"Tossmerflue"!' repeated Xabier, eyeing a figure of Han Solo and diffidently scratching an ear.

I decided it was time for barnyard sounds. 'Let's see,' I said in my most teacherly voice. 'What noises do these animals make? A cow!'

'*¡Mu!*' answered Xabier to my great relief.

'Good! Now how about a dog?'

'*¡Guau-guau-guau!*' barked Xabier in correct Spanish imitation.

No problem there. I decided to go for one more noise. 'Okay, Xabier, now what does a little bird say?'

'*¡Pío-pío-pío!*' Xabier cheeped, again correctly.

I was still stumped. The child was obviously repeating what he had been taught were the sounds of certain animals. Would he have repeated *pío-pío-pío* quite that way if he had not been taught to hear the hatchling's voice so rendered? Nevertheless, he had actually given the standard Spanish rendition for all the sounds I had asked for, so at least he had heard them correctly when he had learned them. And his Spanish speech was perfectly normal.

I decided to wait for a few more classes before saying anything to Xabier's parents and I'm glad I did, for, as the days went by, Xabier began to imitate me faithfully and even to initiate and sustain some basic conversation in English. It had all been a matter of nerves. He got really quite good by the time I left for the States, and I still think of him whenever I hear someone say 'neivi blu!'

In her book *Are You Somebody? The Accidental Memoir of a Dublin Woman*, Nuala O'Faolain describes the bustling pub-life of academic and literary Dublin and its profound educational impact on those who were part of that milieu. Santiago was very similar in the seventies. I had read comparatively little modern literature in Spanish – my degree had been in linguistics – and my year in Salamanca had been enough for a precarious start with isolated novels from different periods and places. I had no firm understanding at the time of the ebbs and flows of literary tastes and genres and an even hazier understanding of the historical connections between the books I had read. But the more intense my social life was, the shorter the many gaps in my knowledge became, for shining nuggets of literary information would somehow materialize in the most incongruous places. For instance, one day, among the spit and sawdust of the Café Reyna, a group of colleagues was discussing the fact German women tourists never seemed to shave their legs or what is today referred to in ads as their 'bikini area'. Some of the women in the group were scandalized.

'It's a terrible shock to see them come out of the water!' one of them wailed.

'Oh, I don't know,' chimed in a chubby, bespectacled woman. 'It's all a matter of what you're used to and the aesthetic your friends follow. Look at Hildegard over in Germanics. When I asked her why she never shaves her legs, she said, "I don't expect my husband to shave his legs, so why should he expect me to?"'

'Mercedes!' we screamed in scandalized unison. 'You actually asked Hildegard why she never shaves her legs?'

'*¡Claro!*' retorted a grinning Mercedes, all mock innocence.

The hesitant Rafael from Literature decided it was time to throw another pebble onto this teetering cairn.

'Well, historically, of course, in some refined circles, hairy women were all the rage,' he began tentatively, shoving his glasses further up his nose.

'What!' we all shrieked at once, a Greek chorus of female respectability.

'Well, not among the ladies of the court themselves,' continued Rafael delicately, 'but, if you remember the *Serranillas* of the Marquis of Santillana, the mountain women of those poems were gigantic types with mustaches whose main virtue seemed to be that they could break you over their backs.'

'¡*Santo cielo!* So they were! But thank God that was four hundred years ago! We're much more civilized now!'

This idle conversation that had started off as a comment on the personal grooming of German tourists was to win me points eleven years later in the Spanish Graduate Record Examinations or GREs. The multiple-choice question was 'Who wrote the *Serranillas*?' The Marquis' name was among the four alternatives offered, and I got away with this and several other questions thanks entirely to gossiping in bars in Santiago de Compostela.

During my first two years in Santiago, I would sometimes be so drained from hours of intense conversation, professionally required or otherwise, that I would duck into shops and bars to avoid greeting friends in the packed streets of the old town. I was learning it was one thing to be talkative by nature and quite another to have to engage people for a living. Nevertheless, I was fascinated by everything I heard and listened avidly to every snippet of chatter for form and context as much as for content. There was one unresolved event, however, that people could not bring themselves to discuss except as isolated incidents in the form of family stories. Language itself had not been forthcoming, so for me to understand the effects of the Spanish Civil War of 1936-39 in terms beyond those of a festering undertow silently tainting all Spanish civil affairs or at most as a lingering, but still searing pain, I would have to be faced with an unprecedented image.

One summer afternoon, some friends from out of town expressed a desire to take a walk down memory lane and visit the Praza do Obradoiro. As we entered the square from the Rúa do Vilar, we decided to have coffee in the café at the exquisite Hostelry of the Catholic Monarchs on the other side, a magnificent hotel built around four inner courtyards, which had once sheltered sick and road-weary pilgrims at the command and expense of King Ferdinand and Queen Isabella. As we sauntered peaceably toward the hotel on that quiet, light-filled Sunday, I wondered aloud at the eerie emptiness of the usually bustling square. José Coira interrupted my question with an urgent outburst.

'¡*Hostia!*'

We all stopped short, training our sights to take in whatever it was he was pointing to. Carlos and Noli gasped.

'What?' I asked, unable to see anything.

But even that was too much. José, Carlos and Noli had all blended into the square's stone silence, frozen in place as if transfixed by a gorgon's head.

At last Carlos broke the spell. 'Look at the top of the double granite staircase,' he muttered, his gray eyes still unable to swerve from the sight. 'Just in front of the entrance to the cathedral.' His wife was wide-eyed, an open hand covering her mouth. He put an arm around her.

I suddenly sensed a somber, crow-like flapping of long black skirts, the agitated darting of a tanned, shiny bald pate atop a light blue shirt, a clumsy, half-toppling windmill of four flailing arms.

'¡*Hostia!*' said José again.

'It's one of the cathedral priests,' I gulped, 'fighting with the local fire chief!'

Everybody turned to look at me, horrified. 'You know him?' they all asked at once.

'The fire chief, yes, not the priest,' I explained hurriedly, still staring at the pair who were battling it out in plain view.

My friends fell silent. The revulsion that emanated from these modern, young, unbelieving Catholics at seeing a priest rain blows on someone was matched only by their shock at seeing someone strike a man of the cloth. It was a scene straight out of one of Buñuel's more surreal films, not something that could possibly happen in the Spain of 1983.

The priest and the fire chief, realizing they had been spotted, disappeared into the cathedral. Shaking at the significance of what we had seen, we continued our walk toward the hotel. Noli was the first to speak.

'So you know the fire chief, eh?' she asked, just to break the silence.

'Yes,' I answered, grateful to be given a candle in this funeral. 'He's a lovely man – collects antique cars and gliders. As friendly as anything.'

'An old *republicano*, for sure,' ventured José, referring to the defeated side in the war. He looked down at his feet, taking hesitant steps.

'I bet the old priest called him a filthy Commie dog,' grinned Noli, 'and that set him off!'

Carlos shook his head. 'Carys,' he said, 'we've just witnessed the reopening of some very old wounds. And, as you've just observed, they're as deep and fresh as when the war ended.'

This brought the conversation to a close, and it was a long time before anybody mentioned the incident again. But I knew

I had seen Spain's bloodiest conflict distilled before my eyes. I had also been present at a disturbing public enactment of a deep-seated taboo: an attack on a priest. The Church, fearing for its future under the democratically elected socialist republic in power in 1936, had aligned itself, much to the sorrow and rage of millions of Spaniards, with the *falangistas*, the side linked to the military insurrection that had sparked the blood-soaked conflagration. The position of the Church thus divided the country even more deeply than the political ravine had, adding one more tragic bead to Spain's traditional rosary of extremist religious and political strife. Unimaginable atrocities were committed by both sides and, even in a time of enforced peace, many pent-up iconoclasts yearned to avenge themselves on a Church they had long considered repressive, retrograde and downright inhumane.

    I knew the fire chief was a worldly, educated man with literary interests, one of the relatively few that had not fled the country at the end of the war. It was striking that such an individual did not hold a more professionally oriented position, but the good jobs, I was told, had all been reserved for those on the winning side. The fire chief was not a man to be bowed by political bullying and had opened a flourishing little souvenir shop in the heart of the old town, where he began to make money hand over fist. He was not to be pigeonholed into the role of the cowed loser: his revenge was to do well and enjoy life, acquiring many of the trappings associated with the winning military government.

    The French physicist Jacques Vallée notes in his memoirs that, as a young man, he left for America to escape the inevitability of social placement he was subjected to in his homeland. Every Frenchman, he said, was accompanied everywhere he went by a metaphorical box that contained the elements of his social standing, education and tastes, and every other Frenchman reacted to him in accordance with what he knew to be the contents of that box. Something very like this was still in effect when I arrived in Santiago in 1974. Everybody could be labeled. At first, I would be angry and astonished when my closest colleague sometimes pontificated on how this or that individual might react to a given situation. His reasoning would be based entirely on a familiarity with the person's walk of life.

'So-and-so isn't telling the truth when he says that the lawyer's daughter threw him over at the last minute and made him lose the deposit,' he announced one day after reading a particular student essay.

'But how do you know that?' I queried, recalling the pleasant, copper-headed young man who had stoically shared that part of his life story with me.

Antonio shook his head sorrowfully. 'Because lawyers' daughters don't move with people like him in the first place,' he answered, the very picture of conviction. This seemed too much.

'But one might have! Have can you be so categorical?' I countered.

'I'm telling you it can't have happened,' sighed Antonio.

I couldn't let him get away with that. I insisted, 'But people are individuals! They can decide on any course of action within their means!'

Antonio gave me his answer roundly enough for me to drop the subject, 'Not here, they can't!'

To my horror (for who wants to believe that people are so transparent?), Antonio was always and inexorably right. He would advise me on what different people's reactions were going to be upon receiving this or that grade, toward this or that politician, what level of society preferred what colors, and he always supported his opinions with minute and perceptive sociohistorical explanations. He himself moved easily within an astonishingly varied array of social circles: regional, national and international. He was also abidingly generous with his knowledge and time. Once it had become clear I'd decided to live in Galicia forever, he would never pass up a chance to help me identify and understand my new countrymen's various identity boxes. Antonio and I would be dancing, for example, at the Don Juan, our frequent haunt on Doutor Teixeiro, and the music would bring us slowly around to a particular vantage point.

'Look now!' Antonio would hiss softly, but urgently, his face taking on an expression of extreme distraction. He would maneuver me so I could include something in my line of vision, in this case an elegant, but soberly dressed young woman on a date.

'Hmm, food for study,' I'd respond happily. 'Looks like an actress playing the glamorous, but very missionary nurse, wouldn't you say?'

'She's a member of the Opus Dei, and you will never see a more illuminating example,' Antonio answered, with a reproving edge to his voice.

'But how can she be religious and dress in that bandbox manner?' I'd wonder aloud, Protestant values to the fore.

'Nothing to do with it. The better dressed she is, the more likely she is to be one of them. They believe in going for the top of the line to show that they understand excellence and impeccable taste as part of God's work. Look at that sexless glamour. She's almost mathematically put together, right out of *Telva*.'

'The fashion magazine? But can a conservative Catholic body like the Opus permit all this attention to such worldly things?'

'My dear, they permit attention to anything at all, as long as it isn't sex!'

'What's their favorite song, do you think?' I'd ask, hoping against hope it would be something hot and heavy.

Antonio would answer without hesitation, '"Longfellow Serenade"!' But the words are quite irrelevant, of course.'

I remembered the ease with which my residence mates in Seville had been able to distinguish the young men who were ex-seminarians, the women who had been nuns, people who were newly rich or recently impoverished. I recalled the care they themselves had taken to appear socially acceptable. One young woman, the daughter of a law professor from Extremadura, had twelve brand-new pairs of designer jeans, fifteen cashmere sweaters and ten pairs of moccasins. All these items were similar in style, but distinct enough not to be taken for any of their closet companions. When I asked her why her wardrobe was so restricted when she could just as easily have purchased more varied and successfully coordinated clothes for the same money, she carefully explained that, since she could never emulate the *marquesas* who came to class every day, dressed from head to toe in never repeated outfits by Dior and Balenciaga, her best strategy for looking expensive was to pretend she was choosing to grace her classes with only the very casual end of a vast and varied wardrobe. Such were the preoccupations of a great number of people. I had yet to realize that, thanks to the Franco regime having successfully incapacitated the more democratic elements of society (the losers in the civil war) by either executing them, causing them to flee the country or denying them important positions in the working world, a well-heeled look was synonymous with political conformity and was therefore safer. All kinds of people were in all kinds of closets.

Looking back now, I am appalled at my willingness to play spot-the-background during my early years in Santiago, however discreetly. It was a skill I had seen perfected by older compatriots in Singapore and Kuala Lumpur, but with different objectives. After my inability or refusal to attach myself to the opportunistic anarchy of Jamaica's shifting emotional terrain, the idea of a people with a series of fixed, predictable and safe outlooks was for a brief moment intrinsically appealing. Innocent though I was of this, the fact the dictatorship had made overt individualism suspect helped me set up categories from which to learn my new world much faster than I would have otherwise, much as grammar serves to present a student with the skeleton of a foreign language. The fleshing out of each person and situation could then be commenced, and the cross-pollinations of taste and character were to become an ever more intriguing discovery.

The battleground on which many nuances of the Galician identity were to be revealed was sociolinguistic. This was the mid-seventies, a period of rich political ferment in Santiago and of a growing examination of the role the Galician identity and language should play in the political and individual life of its citizens. During the Franco regime, under which ideological conformity was often a question of life and death, speaking Galician rather than Spanish was seen as a direct challenge to government authority, if not an encouragement of nationalism. All government business was conducted in Castilian, even with country people who had never spoken a word of that language in their lives. From that stance, it wasn't difficult to put about the notion that Galician was a corrupt half-tongue spoken by peasants whose truncated intelligence prevented them from manipulating the favored structures of Castilian. Wherever, in its evolution from Latin, Galician grammar had deviated from the path taken by Castilian, the difference was attributed to ignorance of correct speech rather than being recognized as a legitimate formation within the family of the Romance languages. Unlike Catalonia, which had sustained a flourishing middle class over several centuries, Galicia, an essentially rural territory, had never been able to wield the political clout necessary to defend its tongue, once the language employed by the court of the scholarly medieval king Alfonso the Wise.

The coerced use of Castilian in a land riven by class prejudice resulted in a jumble of attitudes and aptitudes. Anyone who harbored hopes of reaching or maintaining a position within the realms of the middle classes not only necessarily employed the Castilian language at work, but attempted to adopt it as far as possible at home, in many cases concealing the fact that the first language of the family was actually Galician. Several younger friends of mine, most of whose parents had come to Santiago from smaller provincial towns, told me of a schizophrenic home life in which they would be routinely punished for speaking Galician by parents who employed it themselves as a matter of course. While understanding their parents' desire to prepare them to take professional flight, unfettered by the stigma of 'ignorant' speech, the children themselves were often infuriated by what was sometimes described as entrenched hypocrisy and political cowardice on the part of their elders.

Other children brought up in this type of home, however, inherited the values of their parents, often with bizarre results. One of my friends, the daughter of wealthy parents and heiress to a flourishing business in Santiago, was convinced she not only was unable to speak a word of Galician, but found the language totally impenetrable. Her closest friends, amused at her pretension, knew it was spoken in her household every day. Whatever the reality of her domestic situation, her claim seemed almost surreal. It was common for 'strictly monolingual' society ladies to develop instantly flawless Galician when it came to relaying the sometimes colorful speech of their domestic help.

But this perfect imitation did not count against them socially because Galician was considered beneath serious consideration, like a son's passing dalliance with a shop girl.

Such trivialities notwithstanding, and thanks to changes in attitude brought by the brazen new winds of democracy and the unrelenting work of philologists, sociologists and politicians, ordinary citizens began to realize – or remember – that Galician was a language in its own right, with a glorious, if long buried, literary tradition, not the socially ruinous 'dialect' it had been painted to be. The idea got about that Galicians should be proud to speak Galician if they so wished, in fact that this language best reflected the realities of their homeland. Henrique Monteagudo, a philologist friend of mine, gave me a curious example of this from his own childhood. As a small boy growing up in a fishing village near Fisterra, he had been baffled at the fact his Spanish textbook, aimed at strengthening the vocabulary of the Castilian-speaking pupil, had listed the names of extraordinarily few types of fish – only those familiar to the largely landlocked Castilian population. The result of this neglect of realities beyond the seat of power was later to instill in many Galician children the belief their particular universe was not suitable for representation in schoolbooks. Every child in my friend's class, however, was able to distinguish – and name in Galician – dozens of varieties of fish, which they saw unloaded each day at the docks as their fathers and uncles came home with the day's catch. On one occasion, in response to a question from their teacher as to how many species of fish they could name, the children, thrilled to be on home ground, began to call out the names of the different fish they knew not mentioned in the book. To their bewilderment, the teacher rebuked them for using Galician and reminded them that only Castilian was allowed in class. When asked what the Castilian terms were for the forbidden Galician words, she remained mysteriously silent. Situations like this planted the idea in many puzzled young minds that the officially designated language, though necessary for advancement, did not cover enough bases in the real world.

A later linguistic phenomenon – the stampede of well-intentioned, Castilian-speaking bourgeois professionals struggling to acquire the chic aura of the newly sanctioned language – became a source of rueful amusement. People rushed to learn lists of Galician words, particularly those containing the shushing 'x' sound or a non-Castilian diphthong, or those they could employ in the heady circles of the politically progressive, words often hastily and obviously adapted from Castilian. Adopting Galician was now for many a sign not only of political bravery, but also of upward mobility. It declared to the world that one was open-minded and educated, engaged in righting past wrongs by attempting to forge a more socially equitable state, a state in which (naturally, in view of the degree of radicalism required) the brave new Galician speaker would be accorded a highly visible position in the country's burgeoning democracy.

Many new *galeguistas* were totally ignorant of the fact there were other differences between Galician and Castilian than merely lexical ones. The result was that their utterances were composed of Galician words in a framework of Castilian grammar. The mirror image of this mangled idiom spoken mainly by the elite was the long established and much ridiculed *castrapo*, a sort of pidgin consisting of Castilian words and underlying Galician grammar, spoken largely by recent migrants from the rural areas or 'deserters of the plow' as they were sometimes called. At the heart of the use of this sanitized version of Galician lurked an illicit desire *not* to be taken as a born Galician speaker: after all, in such a fiercely clannish society, where the correct background was paramount, who could afford to have one's listeners think one came from peasant stock? The subtly underlying wish to avoid this fate became evident when it came to the pronunciation of those Galician words that require an open 'e' or 'o' (non-existent in Castilian) such as *quere* and *porta*. For years the interjection of these open vowels into Castilian speech had caused refined ears to flinch because these sounds were not heard as correct phonetic elements of an existing language, but as the uncouth efforts of folk who simply could not contrive to use a 'purer' idiom. The phonetics of the new elite, therefore, were studiously not Galician, so much so that many of my philologist friends, all born speakers, were mistakenly convinced the open vowels were extremely difficult for outsiders to achieve. The fact I had no difficulty with these particular vowels earned me, I ruefully suspect, a point or two in their estimation.

Despite their irritation at the trendy posing taking place around them, during this period one sensed a deep-rooted satisfaction among traditional Galician speakers. Thousands of people felt a huge sense of relief at being able to speak to their babies in the language that sprang first to their hearts without needing to be concerned for the infants' futures. Not least among these new-found pleasures was the knowledge that a whole way of life, an entire Galician identity, was being not only vindicated, but upheld as true and desirable. The feeling of profound personal liberation was for many a hallmark of the times.

The use of the Galician language provided a complex network of sociolinguistic codes by which its speakers (and non-speakers) recognized the fast multiplying subtleties of each other's social and political provenance and aspiration: in other words, their new identity boxes. Added to this was the savage internecine fighting between those who believed that the written standard to be adopted should follow Castilian orthographical trends and those who favored the Portuguese. The lines drawn between *lusistas* and *castelanistas* were markedly political, the former group upholding as its main standard Galician's historically close linguistic relationship to Portuguese, while the *castelanistas* defended the idea that, given Galicia's current identity as part of the Spanish nation and the great influence of the Castilian mainstream upon it, there was a solid practical and historical-linguistic argument in favor of *castelanismo*. The argument was further politicized by the fact that a considerable number of *lusistas* was known for its hatred of all things 'Spanish' and called for the total secession of Galicia from the Spanish state, whereas the *castelanistas* were content to develop a greater degree of autonomy under the umbrella of a loosely federalized Spain. It was this larger group that won the upper hand in the conflict, from which teams of linguists under the direction of pioneering figures compiled the meticulous linguistic atlases, lexicons and grammars out of which a standard Galician language was finally forged and presented to the world in 1982 as *Normas ortográficas e morfolóxicas do idioma galego*.

The Galician that resulted from these efforts was in many respects a language of compromise. Like any other language, Galician displayed from region to region a variety of dialectal and other differences, and the members of the Instituto da Lingua Galega were faced with many difficult decisions as to which word, grammatical structure or pronunciation should be taken as the standard. Whatever choice they made became a potential minefield of controversy. Puzzled or irate citizens were eternally calling them on the telephone, writing to them or stopping them in the street to complain, '*Iso non é a miña fala*' ('That's not my language') or '*Na miña terra dise desta outra maneira*' ('Back home we call this something else'). A patient explanation would ensue as to why the offending form had been adopted. Public interest was enormous. Galician classes for beginners and native speakers were packed to the gills, and the many television and radio programs dealing with language matters were avidly watched and discussed. I finally abandoned the Galician class I was attending out of the most excruciating embarrassment. I felt sorry for the poor teacher known to one and all by his interesting surname of Xove. He was inevitably besieged by challenging and often belligerent questions as to why such-and-such a thing was not considered correct. Accustomed to the absolutism of the strict prescriptive rulings of the Real Academia de la Lengua Española, which, in imitation of its French forerunner, demanded total linguistic obedience in public speech and writing, Galicians believed official non-acceptance of a certain term would ensure its relegation to the nether world of the socially unacceptable. It was difficult to persuade people that no reprisals would ensue if they continued to employ their preferred regional terminology in everyday life and the new recommendations were merely a reflection of the official standardized language. Because of all this, I sometimes had the impression in class I was eavesdropping on a family quarrel in which disappointment, resentment and even fear seemed to cast a pall over people's desire to learn correct Galician and 'I've spoken this language since I was a child, and now it turns out it's not real Galician anymore' was the distressed subtext of their questions. I felt I would be better off not intruding. I had my own identity box to wrestle with and wasn't quite ready to shoulder the emotional heft inherent in that melodious tongue.

By the time I left Santiago, I had learned a great deal of Spanish and finally succumbed sufficiently to the blandishments of the Galician language that I was able to speak it reasonably decently at a pinch. I was a little troubled by the fact I was still a long way from being error-free and didn't have many options as far as vocabulary was concerned, but I had made the leap. Thanks to both languages (and to the English that gave me my living), I had attached myself to more close friends and acquaintances than I could ever have thought possible. My tiny (illegal, as it turned out) attic flat was situated above an apartment inhabited by five kindly, rambunctious operating-room nurses, great comrades all, with whom I interacted on a daily basis and whose living quarters were always filled with friends from the hospital. A couple of feet below them lived a nestful of extroverted, clearly eccentric, young air traffic controllers, two of whom were very close friends of mine. Apart from my own students, and some of the younger academics from Philosophy and Letters and their friends, I had worked closely with a diverse group of physicians and the family and friends of most of the above. There were also my political cronies, and the shopkeepers whose establishments I visited regularly. Keeping the linguistic home fires of my parents' long-time residence in Yorkshire ablaze, I would gabble well into the night with my bosom pal and former student Karen Duncan, a naturalized Spaniard whose childhood had been spent in Sheffield. We would talk about everything under the sun, but mostly about words and phrases, men and relationships, plugging in juicy Yorkshire and Galician expressions among our basic Spanish or English and roaring with laughter at the unholy, but highly satisfying linguistic messes we made. During those years, I talked more and more variously than I could ever have imagined and wrote just as voraciously. I was given the precious chance to eavesdrop on a million modes of speech and twists of language on every subject imaginable. In an outcropping that surprised me, I published a couple of articles in Spanish in the local paper and, thanks to the help and encouragement of Henrique Monteagudo, a couple of Malaysian vignettes in Galician for a literary journal called *Dorna*. From my chair and mentor, Manolo Míguez, I received finely nuanced lessons in how to take possession of a Spanish that reflected a self I was beginning to recognize, as well as years of friendship more generous than I could ever deserve. I was speaking Spanish in my own voice.

Despite – or perhaps because of – the welter of linguistic fascination in which I was immersed, I was still unable to separate physical attraction from language. The men who fought the good fight in the Galician wars of language were highly glamorous figures to me, men who knew the semantic weight and, more importantly, the emotional pull of each word they uttered, the mystery of each lilt of their intonation. Although I did have a few desultory flirtations with men from other professional fields, I felt unable to engage at a deeper level and quickly became bored with them, hungering to feed on a rich, primal stew of gently simmered linguistic elements that would coalesce to nourish my carefully sheltered erotic flowering. The men I desired, dear friends all, were few and often oblivious because the link between speech and physicality I sought was as elusive as the mental acuity required to express this need. I remained a good comrade-in-arms and, I know, a beloved friend.

Converting experience into language was what I had always sensed the world was about, but, as I reached my thirties, I began to suspect that I needed to choose my own path in life, carving out an active destiny of my own rather than merely pursuing the beauty of what Galicia had offered to me. I had already begun to seek other opportunities in a lackadaisical kind of way when, in 1984, María Amparo, the eldest of the Coira siblings, won a coveted residency at a prestigious Barcelona hospital. She had defeated hundreds of other newly graduated physicians in a nationwide exam for the position, which would give her experience in exactly the highly selective medical field she dreamed of making her own. The explosion of joy among her family, friends and acquaintances did not look as if it was ever going to dissipate. A huge bash was planned in the barn at their rambling country house in Rábade.

In a certain way, Amparo's party marked a milestone for all the Lugo group. People suddenly realized their generation had grown up and they were about to chance their own arms, dispersed within a competitive world where their various talents would be put to the unaided test of earning a living. I realized too that my extended, affectionately privileged studentship had finally run out. Amid the whirling *muiñeiras* and *jotas* danced to Luís Coira's amazing bagpipe band, which included (among other traditional instruments) a curious sort of flat tambourine you tied to your chest and thumped like a drunk gorilla, I managed to snatch a few words with Amparo.

'How does it feel?' I shrieked conspiratorially into her ear.

'Ay, I don't know!' she sighed. 'I just feel numb, as if it can't be happening. I just...' Here she interrupted herself, pointing upward and behind me. '*¡Virgen santa!* Look! There's Franxo doing that dumb trick with the champagne again! Would you just look at that!'

I turned to look up at a stocky, red-curled medical student precariously positioned on a set of stacked chairs, shakily attempting to pour a bottle of very good bubbly into an impossibly high pyramid of crystal glasses atop a large armoire.

Amparo continued, 'He's the biggest klutz on the planet, Carys. Why does he always insist on doing this? I just hope *papá* doesn't catch him!'

Franxo was one of the Coiras' close friends, a wild, fun-loving, eccentric young man from Ourense. He was considered *gafe* (jinxed) by all his friends. He had once lent me his cat for safe keeping during a visit by one of his aunts and, despite my very best efforts, within three days the feline had thrown itself out of an open window to its death nine floors below. In the face of possible depredations by Franxo, it was clear Amparo knew her duty. She reverted immediately to her role as elder caretaker and, in all the hullabaloo, I didn't get another chance that evening to consult her heart.

For once, Franxo's party trick was a roaring success. Amid the cheers that greeted his triumphant descent from the swaying pile of chairs and the hearty singing by one and all of 'Catro vellos mariñeiros', 'A Virxe de Guadalupe' and 'A miña nai e mai-la túa' (the very same beloved shanties I had heard from my bed when I first came to Santiago), I made my final decision to stand up and be counted. By the time a singing duel of ever saucier verses flung between Miguel Anxo and an increasingly emboldened Franxo had crept into the dawn, I knew that, much as I loved Galicia and was loved back, her folk songs were not mine, and nor was her future. That belonged to José Carlos, Candela, the Coiras and all the other young people now melding their own twentieth century with the past of their homeland. By the time Miguel Anxo's voice finally gave out to the relief of all, I had determined on a course of action for the future that had been dropping inconvenient hints in my head for more months than I cared to admit. I would study for a graduate degree in Spanish Literature in the United States and earn my living from my own merits, on an equal footing with other students like myself. I would no longer sell my knowledge of the Queen's English for a living, but take a jump into an unknown world. More importantly, I would stick to the consequences. It would tear me to shreds to leave Galicia, but I would make it happen. After all, I had language aplenty.

The author revisiting the Coira family in Galicia, Spain, in 2005.

The author's wedding to Scott Corrales in 1988.

4 AMERICA: STEP ASIDE, LADY!

Whaddya, whaddya...?

To this day, I can hardly believe how I managed to finalize all the arrangements necessary for my leap across the Atlantic and my acceptance as a graduate student at Rutgers, the State University of New Jersey. Shortly after I had made my life-changing decision at María Amparo's party, I sent off an extremely detailed application packet to Rutgers, which I had chosen because it was close to the Galician community in Newark. Some time later, I received a letter inviting me to attend an interview for a teaching assistantship with Dr Phyllis Zatlin, chair of the Rutgers Department of Spanish and Portuguese, who would be flying to Madrid for that purpose. Little did I know that, years later, Dr Zatlin – in conjunction with her colleague Dr Margaret Persin – would become co-director of my doctoral thesis and, like Dr Persin, a dear friend. I was panicked out of my wits, quite unnecessarily as it turned out. Phyllis gave me the longest and most fascinating interview I had ever experienced, which included a visit to a book fair in the Retiro in Madrid and tea at the home of Elena Quiroga, a well-known Galician author. It was from Phyllis that I learned to my shock that, as a foreign graduate student, I would be expected to take the Graduate Record Examinations or GREs. I misunderstood her to mean that I would have to take them before Rutgers accepted me. Somehow, in the nick of time, I arranged to take the exams and found two students, Paco and Tito, who were planning to drive to Madrid for the same reason and agreed to give me a lift in exchange for sharing the cost of gasoline.

My first view of America was a tiny suburb extravagantly adorned with Christmas lights, fairyland strands of colors such as I had never seen outside a private house. In the energy-scrimping, do-without Europe of 1985, the sight struck the three of us like a slap in the face to a fainting woman: well-meaning, but sharply felt. We had finally driven up to El Encinar de los Reyes, the Royal Oaks housing for the Torrejón Air Base near La Moraleja, north of Madrid, where we were to take our GREs the following morning and were scoping out the terrain in order not to get lost on the morning of the exams.

Back at the flat where a garrulous medical student friend of Tito's had hospitably offered us sleeping space for the night, I realized the yellow, heavy smoke of Celtas that was the main furnishing in that otherwise spotless, white-tiled apartment would not be propitious for a good night's sleep. My hard contact lenses were already killing me, and I knew days of sinusitis would follow a night in that friendly, smog-ridden place. Apart from that, our host was poorly prepared to put up three people who had not thought to bring sleeping bags, towels or anything else. I had noticed a sign drawing attention to an inexpensive-looking *pensión* as we were hauling ourselves up the winding stone staircase. Perhaps I could put my mad money to good use there: at least it would mean one less stranger in the apartment for Germán to accommodate, as well as some privacy for me. So, when bedtime came along, I thanked Germán for his offer of a chair for the night and carefully explained I would be sleeping two floors down at the boarding house. The lads were thunderstruck.

'I just can't imagine that a person would rather stay at a hotel than with friends,' mused Tito resentfully, and I realized I had made it look as if I didn't trust them.

'I'd certainly prefer to stay here,' I lied, 'but I'm allergic to cigarette smoke and, this way, you guys can catch up on old times. I'm sure it'll be much more comfortable for everybody if I'm out of the way.'

When the door of the boarding house opened to my ring, I realized immediately I had stepped into a Madrid to which I would never otherwise have gained entrance. The smiling, middle-aged man behind the rickety front desk was accompanied, height for height, by a life-size poster of a sickeningly smooth, tuxedoed Julio Iglesias. Stuck to the glass front of the counter was another poster, this one advertising Manolita Chen and her *teatro chino*, an emblematic burlesque show that had made 'Chinese theater' synonymous with striptease in the minds of much of the Spanish populace.

Oh, well. What could possibly happen to me, after all? I'd simply flash my well-thinking, good-girl smile at everybody I saw and then lock myself in my room for the night. I'd be out before anybody knew I'd even been there.

'*Buenas tardes*,' I greeted the night porter, who was not looking at all curious to see me. 'Do you have space for one person, just for the one night?'

'Of course,' smiled the man, exactly as if I were a member of the family. 'Just for one person, did you say?'

It occurred to me I had better provide some unsolicited information.

'I'm in Madrid to take an exam tomorrow. I'll have to leave very early in the morning, so can I pay you now?'

'Just as you like,' smiled the man.

We were now joined by a stocky, black-haired man in his thirties, with the stealthy air of a successful stowaway. I now know he must have been among the first of the wave of recent Spanish-speaking Caribbean immigrants making a new life in Madrid, but at the time he seemed a very exotic personage indeed. He bought a blue-and-white pack of Ducados cigarettes, nodded courteously and moved off.

I was shown to a room along a darkish passageway with the strangest configuration of a hostelry I had ever seen. One entered the room through a double-wide, doorless aperture and almost immediately confronted another wall. To either side of me along the wall were twin iron beds facing each other, as it were, toe to toe. These beds made up almost the entire furnishing of the room. Perhaps the place had once been a sanatorium of sorts. The open door space faced the common bathroom head-on across the corridor, which, I was pleased to notice, was about five feet wide. I would have to get undressed in the bathroom and then climb into bed pretty much within sight of anyone passing along the corridor. But it would be a bed and it would be cheap and it was in the same building as my friends. If anything tabloid-worthy happened to me, the world would know how I'd come to be in such a curious place. There was no point in being frightened now. I had paid for my bed and now I was sleeping in it.

Somehow, with one eye open like a hare, I managed to get a good night's sleep. I was woken up once in the very early hours by what looked and sounded in the dim light like an elderly sleepwalker with a deathly, retching cough, painfully making his way down the passage – bolt upright despite the awful coughing – in a slow, hypnotic glide toward the bathroom. He closed the door behind him, his scraping gasps for air now muffled somewhat, but still persistent and distressing enough for me to wonder if I should call the night porter in case he died right there, that night, in the room in front of mine. But his coughing gradually began to lose its intensity, and I fell asleep, not to wake again until my tiny travel alarm clock buzzed me alert at 5 a.m.

When we reached the base that morning, we were two hours early for the start of the exams. But, since we had been told we could not be assured of extra question papers to do all the necessary exams in the first place, we had decided to arrive ahead of time to be first in line. The administration of the exams turned out not to favor this plan, but we had done our best. I had been promised a Spanish exam and a Math, but would have to see if I could do the Analytical and the English as well. Tito and Paco, whose entire futures hung by the fast fraying thread of doing well on the Biology exam, had been promised nothing at all. We were very nervous.

Strolling around the corner of the base to which our instructions had directed us, we noticed a small cinema showing what must have been popular films, and a sort of supermarket. Desperate for something to do to fill in the time before we had to report for our exams, we went in and began to browse the shelves. They were loaded with exotic items such as Aunt Jemima Pancake Mix, cereal, peanut butter, biscuit mix, cake mix. We didn't have a chance to see much more before we were politely and firmly bundled out of the establishment.

'This is a PX,' I was told in English by a stern-looking soldier.

'Civilians can't come in here.'

'I'm sorry!' I answered, abashed. 'What's a PX?'

The clerk stared at me closely. No reply was given.

Paco and Tito were clearly offended. 'Mother of God,' muttered Paco. 'As if anyone would want to steal that crap! Did you see what those Yanks eat? Powder out of boxes, that's what!'

'Now, now, Paco, I'm sure they get plenty of fresh food from the market!' I offered, oil over troubled waters.

'I doubt it,' Paco continued, his black eyes glittering with suspicion. 'If we ever get to America, we're going to starve to death. I can see it now. Hamburgers, hot dogs and sugared cement, that's all they eat. I'm certainly not touching that stuff!'

Wondering how much his attitude was a fence against the possibility of not being able to take the exam, I didn't pursue it. I was too preoccupied with locating the school. As soon as they appeared within my line of sight, I went up to a pleasant-looking, arm-linked couple, she a blond woman in curlers, he upright and handsome in his Air Force uniform.

'*Buenos días,*' I said to them. '*Por favor, ¿dónde queda la escuela primaria?*'

The woman smiled. 'I'm sorry, ma'am,' she answered. 'We don't speak Spanish.' Pointing over my shoulder to the left, she added, 'Maybe they can help you in the PX.'

I was absolutely flabbergasted. I had simply not realized that the military base would be a piece of America, like an embassy. I was even more bewildered by the fact neither individual of the couple could speak such basic Spanish as I had employed when I had addressed them.

'*Malditos imperialistas,*' Paco cursed. '*¿Te fijaste como se negaron a contestarte en castellano?* (Did you see how they refused to answer you in Spanish?) They think the whole world belongs to them!'

By this time, more exam-takers were beginning to arrive. Some of them knew where the school was, so we joined them. Before long, an obese military policeman, hat and all, arrived with a tiny, nervous administrator who looked as if he might have originally been Filipino. I was soon separated from my friends, who were ushered into another line. When my turn came, I was attended to by the MP, who, I realized to my absolute terror, was armed. I had never been so close to an armed individual in my life. His gun seemed enormous, threatening. It looked alive, glittering as it was in that clear Madrid light. What was an armed person doing signing me up for an exam? I began to feel very jittery.

As it turned out, the MP was friendly enough. 'A Brit, eh?' he asked, smiling knowingly. 'I'm from West Virginia myself.'

'Oh, really?' I beamed, trying to look harmless.

'Why's a British woman like you fixin' to learn Spanish in the States?' he continued in a slightly sardonic tone, although it was clear he was truly puzzled. Something about the way he pronounced the word 'woman' – 'womman' – signaled to me that no answer I could possibly give would be satisfactory.

I flashed my most charming smile. 'America has great graduate schools in Spanish literature,' I said reassuringly. 'The best!'

'Well, I'll be doggone,' he concluded. 'Go figure!' Then he jabbed a stubby forefinger at the examination room and wished me good luck.

When my first exam was doled out with a yellow pencil, I was stunned. A pencil! I hadn't used a pencil to write with since I was six and graduated to pens. One look at the questions, and I knew I had been whisked into another dimension. We were given four possible answers to each question and, at the side of each choice, was the tiny outline of an egg. Risking the displeasured might of the MP from West Virginia, I shot a guilty glance at the candidates to my left. They were feverishly filling in the little eggs with their pencils. Humiliated at being asked to take part in such an activity, I lowered my head and began to read.

'To what Latin American civilization does the pyramid in the illustration belong?' The choices were: 'Inca', 'Maya', 'Toltec' and 'Aztec'.

Eighteen years later, my husband was to tell me he had taken exactly the same exam and the correct answer had been 'Maya'. By that time, I had taken several specialized courses in Latin American literature and had viewed several famous Mayan and Toltec structures for myself. At that moment, however, I felt the bottom of my stomach fall and my head become light as if it too were about to detach itself from my anatomy. Questions on literature and culture! I had been led to believe in the absence of a sample exam that the whole test would be on language alone! 'I am not prepared,' I thought and then corrected myself. 'I am prepared! Prepared to fail!'

As it turned out, my general reading and all those years of gabbing in Spanish cafés and at dinner parties with talkative friends had stood me in good stead. I did creditably well on all my exams except Math, where, despite loyal coaching by my friend José Carlos, I made the 12th percentile. Fortunately the Department of Spanish and Portuguese at Rutgers didn't seem to care much.

When I finished the grueling round of tests, I staggered, half blind from filling in eggs, into the crisp air. I found Paco and Tito waiting at the car as we had arranged. Paco was visibly irritated.

'What took you so long?' he inquired petulantly. 'We've been waiting for you for hours!'

'Why? What about your…?'

'We never took the exam,' Paco replied, throwing away his cigarette. 'There was only one copy left.'

My heart sank. 'Oh, no! What an awful thing to have happen! But *one* of you took it, right?'

A jagged-edged silence ensued.

'But didn't you toss a coin?'

'No,' came Tito's hollow voice from inside the car. 'They asked us to, but we refused.'

I sat down on the sidewalk, crestfallen. I knew there was nothing I could say to alleviate the fury and disappointment brought by that grand gesture of these two friends, who had each given up their only stab at a dream in case the other were left behind. They were back to the privation of chronic unemployment and hardship, knowing that a bright future would have shone for them had it not been for the other.

It was a very, very long ride back to Santiago. Whereas the route down had forged a rapid friendship, crammed as it had been with excited conversation, maudlin singing and political speculation, Paco and I cowered in a kind of brutalized silence. Tito tried to drown his sorrows by singing tangos under his breath, his monotonous voice like soft marbles as the words loped out of his throat. This aggravated Paco beyond bearing and in his devastation he called Tito an animal and the mother that brought him forth the great whore. During the whole journey back to Santiago, he continued verbally to defecate on Tito, the Holy Eucharist and the mother's milk that Tito had suckled as a babe. Luckily I had heard all this language a million times before or I would have had to jump out of the car.

A couple of years later, I heard that Tito had won a very coveted teaching position in a local high school, a post that had been up for very fierce public competition, and Paco had secured a place as a teaching assistant at the biology department of a prestigious American university, so they had both landed on their feet. I have no idea if they are still friends.

Before I was able to take stock of all the preparations necessary for my leap across the Atlantic, I found myself deplaning at Newark Airport one August morning, drenched instantaneously by the steam in the atmosphere. It was the muggiest day I had ever experienced since Malaysia. The first previously landed Americans I saw as I walked toward the baggage claim were two huge Hasidic Jews complete with curly side-hair and oddly sitting ermine hats that looked as if they were about to spring from their heads and make a run for it in the strangely thrown together atmosphere of that terminal. I quickly found my way amid a squawking souk of vying barkers touting different types of public transportation including the 'limousines' mentioned in my now crumpled and sweated-out instructions from Douglass College. The 'limousines' turned out to be more like battered milk vans than ostentatious wedding conveyances. As I surrendered to an affable, unintelligible driver my two suitcases – the newest one a present from my father – I made a last-ditch attempt to verify we were indeed bound for New Brunswick, and my trip to my new home started on its noisy way. Our unairconditioned rattle-trap was stuck in that heat wave for two hours in a traffic jam opposite a drum farm, but I was still thrilled. At the New Brunswick Hyatt, I unwrinkled my half-sheet of paper and scanned it for the telephone number I needed to summon the person from Douglass College who was to drive me to campus. This was a meaty, red-haired, summer work-study student whose total indifference to my circumstances and excitement at being in America verged, I thought, on the perverse. I was in awe of the historic step I had made, she was on pick-up detail. But I had already been blessed by a nice, garrulous lady waiting behind me to use the telephone at the hotel.

'Be safe,' she told me. Then, increasing her good wishes by several degrees of emphatic urgency, she added, 'And get a good job.'

Be SAFE? Is this what people wished each other in the Promised Land? Get a good JOB? Where was my immortal soul in all of this? Where was 'be happy'? 'Be free'? Where was 'get to know the real Carys'? I was a little miffed as we gave each other a ceremonial kiss goodbye.

'Oh, well,' people were to tell me later, 'that's Noo Joisey!'

For the next four years, America took on the shape of the various Rutgers campuses linked in part by George Street, New Brunswick, and the area to the north occupied by Sears. I was very fortunate to have been offered the positions of Director of the Casa Hispánica at Douglass College, a residential post, and Teaching Assistant in the Department of Spanish and Portuguese. I was to earn my living by teaching an elementary Spanish course for the department and running the Spanish House, which meant organizing a plethora of activities as well as teaching a cultural class in-house. This was how I was to pay my way through a Master's in Spanish Literature and later, if all went well, a doctorate. What all this meant for the future, I had no idea. I was blissfully ignorant of what teaching in the US involved, had no idea of the tenure process, no idea of the publish-or-perish ethos, no idea of life in America, no real idea of the intellectual package with which the average American high-school graduate is equipped, no idea of the credit-gathering approach to learning, no idea of the world beyond the campus, no idea of anything. Today, I quake in retrospect at the ignorance of my ignorance. But at the time it mattered little: my goal was to start from scratch, to grow into reality, to grow into myself out of new soil. I'd make a livable world around me.

My first impression of the deserted Douglass Campus that August – the great mass of students had not yet begun to arrive – was of great tranquility and beauty slashed through with fear. The nucleus of the campus was made up of a handful of handsome old buildings, with parkland surrounding new student and teaching buildings and a meltingly beautiful library, all landscaped with a purposeful grace. Plastered all over the inside of the Spanish House, which formed part of a sunny, airy new building on the edge of campus, were garish notices warning residents of intruders, of the dangers of rape by outsiders or their dates, of armed strangers. Accustomed to walking around Santiago at all hours of the day and night in perfect safety, the pervasive smell of violence in this manicured, apprehension-smeared paradise put a stamp of sickening terror on my immediate terrain and the new country that circled it. I felt restricted in a way I had never experienced before.

When I mentioned this to an American teaching assistant once classes had begun, she gave a deprecatory wave of the hand. 'Oh,' I was told. 'Pay no attention to all that stuff on the walls: that's only there because of lawsuits. You have to warn everybody about absolutely everything or parents will sue Rutgers for whatever they can.'

Friends in Spain had often laughed at the fact that every product used by Americans had advisories of dreadful danger printed upon it and Americans needed to be warned not to spray fly-killer in their eyes or drink toilet declogger. 'Who but an American would be dumb enough to think of squirting fly-spray into their eyes?' people would ask, doubled over with mirth.

It occurred to me that warnings about rapists must be part of the same syndrome, especially as the Douglass College administrators and faculty members I met were immensely solicitous, kind and generous, inviting me to their homes, ice-cream parlors and shopping malls. On the day after I arrived, the head of the Douglass alumnae – into whose office I had stumbled, half starved, mapless and looking for a place to buy food – handed over her well-balanced lunch with a welcoming smile.

The anti-rape flyers were not the only papers that made their mark upon the unwary stranger. Rutgers bureaucracy was a dehumanizing aspect of the institution that caused the foreign students profound distress. The immense weight of the paperwork involved merely to enroll in classes was mind-blowing to me, accustomed as I was to the seat-of-the-pants methods of Spanish university administration. Because this paper chase took place across several campuses, we fast learned from our American fellows the meaning of the verb 'to schlep'. For us Carpender-dwellers (the Spanish and Portuguese Department was housed in that endearing Victorian structure on the Douglass campus), chasing down the papers included the drudgery of traveling by the (free, thank goodness) Rutgers bus service to the administrative building on the faraway Busch campus. This was a strange and unusual punishment for those of us used to dashing about on foot, for whom travel in a conveyance was an option, not a necessity. The staff at the vilified administration building were always overwhelmed with work and therefore sometimes lacked the patience for extra explanations, especially for people with foreign accents who themselves were stressed beyond endurance from listening to entire dayfuls of rapid-fire English conversations.

Although I was mercifully spared some of the aggravation related to dorm existence because of the very nice apartment provided for me by the terms of my contract as Director of the Spanish House, I noticed that another source of worry for foreign graduate students was the nagging fear they had unknowingly committed an infringement on the conditions of residence life. Before we arrived at our assigned dorms, we had all been the recipients of reams of instructions and threat sheets regarding life in a residence hall. We were instructed as to exactly what one could and could not do, what would and would not be provided, precisely what electrical gadgets (several, like the ubiquitous hot pot, totally unknown to us) would cause one to be in bad odor with the fire marshal and the college. It seemed we were forbidden more appliances than we had ever heard of. There were rules and regulations about room-mates and the changing thereof, meal plans, and, once we arrived on campus, seas of flyers about acquiring carpets, potted plants, posters, how to decorate a college dorm room, how to live with a roommate, how to manage time, how to handle stress. The greatest difficulty was that, unlike our American classmates, we had no experience in recognizing the identity of each piece of paper as it arrived. Every sheet had to be read carefully before we could make a decision as to whether or not it was important or could be ignored, whereas the American graduate students would just glance through the daily pile, throwing colored paper away with abandon. The strain was enormous.

For foreigners, there was one further hurdle: getting all one's paperwork in order as regards immigration, student visas and suchlike. At the center for overseas students on College Avenue, the staff were as different from the exhausted denizens of the Busch administrative buildings as they could possibly be. Despite their courteous and good-humored efforts with these frantic, culture-shocked students, the place always seemed to be a nightmarish interspersion of queues and incorrect documentation punctuated by unnervingly loud notices about observing the American custom of line-forming. The woman in charge of that office should have been beatified in life. I once saw her offer to lend money from her own pocket to a foreign TA who had not been advised that his first salary would take two months to process instead of the four weeks he had so tightly budgeted for. Those of us who were also teaching assistants had to get our classes together with the attendant paperwork, meeting several times with our new colleagues to make sure all sections were taught in a concerted manner.

Life at the Casa Hispánica was wonderful, at least for this director. The house had a capacity for twenty-four students and was always full. The ideal was that all conversation in the public areas of the house would be conducted in Spanish and students would attend a weekly cultural class taught by me. They would eat a certain number of meals a week at the Spanish Table in a certain area of the Douglass College dining room that was restricted to cultural house members and their guests. All this Spanish speaking was carried out, as the expression goes, *mal que bien*, as some students were more fluent than others, but they did participate enthusiastically in our events. I decided to eschew all the pop-culture images of Hispanic life – bullfights, piñatas, etc. – and attempted to expose them to as many Spaniards and Latin Americans as I could. I organized visits by two very different Cuban poets, a Manhattan social worker, a young Puerto Rican couple who taught us to do the salsa, a Puerto Rican ecologist, an Argentinian feminist writer, the mayor of a Central American city, a Spaniard teaching in New York, a Mexican student from Cuernavaca, an American Borges expert, a Puerto Rican feminist poet and sundry others. We also set up a scholarly panel discussion to commemorate the anniversary of Rosalía de Castro's death, several showings of avant-garde Spanish-language films and a number of train trips in the freezing cold to see different plays performed by the Repertorio Español in Manhattan. We were lucky to have the Big Apple with all its

Hispanic offerings so close at hand. Once a year, to my horror, the cultural houses had to put on a morning of entertainment to coincide with an International Weekend the deans had instituted. Preparation for this event never failed to make my flesh creep, for, despite the very forward-looking policies of the Douglass administration, there was an inescapable 'bring on the dancing girls' air about their expectations for the weekend. It soon became clear that, in those early days, their idea of showcasing the cultural houses had more to do with a fifties-style pageant with exhibitions of colorful, whirling skirts and stomping feet than it did with anything else. I tried diplomatically to voice my suspicions that their view of the cultural-house show was a far cry from their solid feminist aspirations for the rest of the college, but I don't think my explanations sank in. What else could a cultural house do but a song-and/or-dance routine or some good international cuisine? In the end, we would put on skits we hoped illuminated certain cross-cultural problems, or bilingual poetry readings linked to special events. It was dreadful to see the Mickey-Mouse level of some of the exhibits, however, most of which served to emphasize the time-worn stereotypes already prevalent: the arm-waving, pizza-house Italian, the swaggering Spaniard, the lederhosen-clad, clodhopping German dancers, the French girls in regulation black berets and horizontally striped T-shirts, the babushkas... It was an uphill battle. The one truly memorable exhibit was staged the year I left by the Asian House: a demonstration of Chinese calligraphy by a swift-armed young woman with a flip chart, who had to work faster and faster as the crowd demanded more and more elegant black ideograms for their dorm walls.

    Douglass College had for years been an independent establishment for young women, until it was subsumed by the long arms of the Rutgers octopus in 1968. Nevertheless, in 1985, its campus retained its particular traditions, a certain redolence of the East-Coast establishment, and its energetic administration headed by the beloved Mary Hartman. It had also done a wonderful job in stoking a feminist outlook and providing excellent educational opportunities for its young women. Outstanding women from many professions, often national and international celebrities, were regularly invited to the campus, and it was as a result of a particular panel discussion including such disparate spirits as New Zealand's Marilyn Waring and *Now*'s Robyn White that I first became enthused by the differing political voices of dialogue among women. I was also honored to meet Charlotte Bunch and Paula Giddings.

The Rutgers Department of Spanish and Portuguese was nothing if not hectic in those days, infused by the must-have-it-all spirit of the eighties. Stocked as it was with national experts in many fields striving to add to their already impressive CVs and thronged with bright, young (and not so young) teaching assistants whose lives depended entirely upon their grades and how many departmental activities they could cram into their desperate lives, Carpender House was in ferment. Keeping one of the precious teaching assistantships involved maintaining the highest possible grades, presenting at least one term paper per semester at a scholarly conference or – marvel of marvels – actually getting one published in a reputable journal. In addition, one had to have reasonably good teaching evaluations from students. The department was very careful to mentor us in this area in preparation for our futures as young academics. It added to one's reputation to be seen at all film showings, guest lectures and local conferences and particularly to play a visible role in – or, better still, to organize – some educational event. One didn't have to be a personable representative of a particular ethnic group, but it certainly looked better if one were. This punishing milieu was my entire world: I had no other. I was determined not to complain – I had always despised the expatriates in Malaya who thought only in critically acrid terms about the country where they were guests – and I was desperate not to fail, not to make the burning of my Santiago boats all for naught. I worked like a demon, juggling all the above with duties at the Spanish House and teaching within the department, my parched soul thirsty for A grades. On top of this, I accepted every extra invitation discovered of a morning in my departmental mailbox to present at this, advise on that and help amuse this other visiting writer or playwright. I was a squirrel on a scurrying wheel, eternally running, but clueless as to where the wheel would lead. During my first year, I accepted this as life in America, aware of nothing but the need to keep the wheel turning from event to event, term paper to exam to class presentation. It didn't occur to me it was possible to do less, to be an average graduate student, even an average TA. I certainly didn't see all the events to which I subjected myself as opportunities to learn and enhance my career, opportunities not open to students at lesser universities with lower profiles, far away from the fertile, all-consuming spread of Manhattan. What would happen to me if I failed to make a rewarding new life for myself? The prospect was the abyss. To me, these obstacles meant I would blandly have to whip up even more flagging energy, husband even more gracious good will, count out even more desperately measured hours. Looking back at those days from the perspective of a college professor at a friendly and aspiring rural school, I sometimes long for even a fraction of the flying mosaic of events and resources Rutgers was able to offer its students at that time.

 I now realize other battles were being waged around us: battles for the allegiance of the most promising TAs, who would later turn into desirable doctoral students; battles for the creation of 'schools' among us unknowing fish; and, most savage of all, battles to wrest prestige and therefore funding from the visible heads of rival specializations. Fortunately we small fry were for the most part much too busy to notice a great deal of this, and the notion we were being tagged as eminent scholars of the future would have been the last straw. But the TAs did not suffer the worst of the academic spinning wheel. We witnessed the demoralizing effect on our instructors as they waited for tenure decisions taken, as I understood it, by committees not necessarily specialized in each candidate's subject. If they were denied tenure, they would be given one more year before they had to give up their jobs and go through the grueling process of applying for a position at another university. This was made even more heartbreaking by the fact they would surely be quizzed on why they had left the excellent school they had been part of. Luckily, one lecturer who was not awarded tenure when I was there was welcomed with open arms by another well-known university, whose Spanish department was as puzzled as we were that she had been turned down at Rutgers.

Meanwhile, a strange, disjointed tarot-spread of curiously fascinating linguistic cards was being dealt before me. I picked them up one by one, weighed their effect on different dimensions of my life as it then stood, and surveyed the entire throw as a unit to see if it would form some kind of pattern. It never did.

In a recent CNN interview, I was excited to hear the linguist John McWhorter observe that he was currently writing a book about the origins of the informality of American English. I can hardly wait to read it because the most astonishing thing I noticed about my new campus nation during my first semester was a speech by the Rutgers president, so very different from those given by the departmental and Douglass College dignitaries.

Dr Bloustein's grammar was haphazard, his vocabulary and intonation no different from those employed by most people for transactional purposes at a local carwash, except that he was clearly a native speaker of English. I was stunned. In no way did the register of his speech match the dignity of the situation. Nobody else seemed as taken aback as I, and those I asked thought I was criticizing the man for some used-car salesman conduct or other. It soon dawned on me our president had only one suit of linguistic clothes, a suit he wore all the time. I felt somehow cheated. I wanted the emperor to have a special robe I could study and admire. Malays have different sets of vocabulary, deployed for different situations, and the British recognize registers that can be taken up and put down again like objects on a shelf. Why were the Americans so impoverished in this respect?

I was to see this a lot during the following years and came to understand it was desirable in a human being: acting like a chameleon was frowned upon as untrue to one's self, manipulative and possibly indicative of criminal intent. Politicians, I was told, took particular care not to lose their regional accents – 'you have to sound like where you're from' – although upwardly mobile individuals from markedly recognizable cities like Pittsburgh sometimes found it expedient to go to elocution classes to wash away any chance of being spotted as a 'yinzer'. Although I did not see myself as a person given to particularly recondite vocabulary, I was constantly questioned about this or that item from my lexicon, often by academics. The simplicity of most public announcements astonished me until I was told that by law no commercial instruction booklet or public sign could be couched in language beyond that considered the level of a tenth grader, that is to say beyond the level attained by an individual leaving school at the earliest possible legal age. The logic of this glares like the sun on the newly tarmacked road of practicality.

In New Jersey, where a great deal of immigration from Europe took place, the point of language was to get things done, to negotiate jobs and prices, to invite neighbors over for a beer. Speaking English meant knowing enough to put food on the table and a roof over the children's heads. Speaking good English meant doing so without a foreign accent, being a good long step away from the old country. Levels of connotation and insinuation, it seemed to me, simply did not come into the picture for most people. Then someone lent me *The Joys of Yiddish*, and language began to laugh out loud once more. Leo Rosten's book had my mind doing somersaults over the countless, finely differentiated terms for psychological human types, not to mention the uproarious differences between a 'schlemiel', a 'schlimazel' and so on. Curiously the word 'schmaltz' originally referred to chicken fat and later came to denote a certain kind of overdone sentimentality where English might have employed a term linked to syrup. (The fact that an old Spanish word meaning chicken fat – *enjundia* – is used to refer to great scholarship is also intriguing. What is it about chicken fat that cures what ails you?)

Amongst the teeming races for more engagements, more articles, more chances for the students to deepen and broaden their vita-molded knowledge in an aggressive, pointy-shouldered, Spandex-aerobic America that scorned those who hesitated to have it all, there was one single grain of self-restraint: political correctness. We worked in a kind of linguistic trance, avoiding all mention, however innocent, of gender, gender preference, skin color, sociological background and religion. Though it was acceptable to tell a colleague certain students were smart or hardworking, one had to avoid referring to them by any term that could be interpreted as meaning the opposite. We studiously taught ourselves to conceive of everyone as clones. This meant that, while nobody was unfairly discriminated against, there was little joy in our differences, little mirth over linguistic usages, little wonder in the human spirit, for the simple reason it was considered improper to refer to anything that might be conceived as differentiating an individual against a norm. But if an individual cannot be individualized, how can a person be a person? How can true diversity flourish if we are all to aspire to considering everyone as not just equal in rights, but the same in every other way? Here the Spanish word *igual* comes to mind, signifying as it does both 'equal' and 'the same'. Do the PC guidelines mean that, as well as enjoying equal rights, we must also be the same? We can't be. Indeed, we mustn't be. This is something Diane Ravitch points out in her book *The Language Police*, along with other curiously horrifying educational strategies such as the avoidance in textbooks and standardized exams of references to anything that might upset anyone. Thus, no mention of Satan or senility, and it appears there is an injunction against old persons being portrayed as wearing glasses or using walkers. The carved presidential faces of Mount Rushmore, for example, should not be mentioned or portrayed because they have been hewn out of land that is sacred to the Lakota Sioux. In the name of the avoidance of stereotyping, no particular group can be depicted or described with any detail that distinguishes them from any other, and no comparative references can be made to any human group or nation lest the writer be seen as imposing a norm. This is all very well and good, but it has the ghastly effect of depriving American schoolchildren of a great deal of information about the world. It's a case of a much needed baby being thrown out with the bathwater and a serious act of historical revisionism. Would it not be in the better interests of all parties to describe Mount Rushmore, but point out the carvings were carried out to the great distress of the Lakota Sioux? A certain early African-American educationalist was left out of a particular text because she was separated from her husband and themes such as divorce and separation were deemed too upsetting or ideologically incorrect for some children to have to encounter in schoolbooks and tests.

All this denial of things that exist in the world is dangerous enough for the deprivation it brings to our children without the fact many Americans receive nearly all their knowledge from formal coursework. Apart from the traditional skills acquired from one's home community and the religious instruction given in churches, temples and mosques, many, many people know nothing beyond what they have been officially taught by a paid educator. I cannot remember how many times I have been asked (sometimes by academics) how it is I know so much about anthropology, world religions, etc. My husband, who is neither an historian nor a sociologist, is repeatedly asked where he went to school for medieval history, sociology, etc. Although the advent and widespread use of the Internet have done wonders to broaden all our educations in every single subject one could hope to read about and an infinite number of those one would rather not, the fact remains that knowledge in America is pretty much acquired on a need-to-know basis that is often purely transactional. ('How much do I need to know to earn three credits?') Sadly the knowledge itself is often dispensed on a similar basis, like carefully measured drops from a bottle of medicine. ('What's the minimum amount of work I need to teach this sorry crew at this particular academic level?') The result of this measurement of the worth of knowledge is that some students are annoyed at having to think the extra thought and resentful of students who are keen to do so. All this causes hassles for instructors come grading time. ('How do I give credit for original thinking or for independent reading? How do I explain to the uninterested student why he or she did not get the grade expected although he or she attended every class and did every assignment correctly?') The answer is that, in the interests of 'fairness', the mechanical-minded student all too often gets the same grade as one who went far beyond the minimum.

Very frequently, especially in grade school, a certain dumbing down of student work is implemented so that testing can be more 'fair', the aim being not to ask questions that cannot be graded on standardized tests or may allow a particular student's superior knowledge, acquired out of class, to creep into the otherwise sanitized testing system. Thus, teachers dislike hearing children using terms that are not 'vocabulary words', a description that invariably makes me cringe, which refers to the list of words prescribed for that child to know at his or her level. It seems to me it is one thing to avoid unfairness by not asking anything beyond a prescribed area, but quite another to penalize students for wider knowledge.

As a teacher of a second language (we mustn't say 'foreign' anymore because that would be ethnocentric, despite the fact any second language, compared to the first, is usually foreign, which is why we are having to learn it in the first place), I have become very much aware of the implications of this measured compartmentalization of instruction for our students. Students tend not to realize that Spanish (or any other language) is a roiling sea of syntax, vocabulary dancing an intricate jig in an untold number and placement of registers, and wildcat elements such as idiom, metaphor, irony, intertextuality and so on. They believe that Spanish is what is contained in the chapters of the class text that will be covered in any given semester. They would therefore prefer to employ only the grammar and vocabulary in the next text, heaving everything they have learned since the last exam overboard. New port, new cargo, splash! The results are sometimes quite comical as students attempt to gain fluency in a certain tense while forgetting every other tense they ever learned. (This week I can speak about parts of the body in the future tense, next week I'll speak about banking in the conditional, etc.). Wise authors of textbooks have been onto this trick for years now, and modern texts are beautifully organized to include all tenses and fields of vocabulary presented with software that includes video clips of contextualized conversations from real life that can be played over and over again, supplemented by dictionaries (some of them visual) and grammatical explanations from which information can be summoned at the touch of a key. Despite all these marvels, students are sometimes annoyed at having to remember everything at once, accustomed as they are to dealing with one concept at a time.

The need-to-know concept applied to people as well, I soon found. Before I left for America, I was told by a Santiago colleague, 'You'll find that Americans are not at all interested in who you are, only in what you can do.'

At the time, I took this to be some kind of a reflection on the democratic ideals of a new nation, a reference to America's rejection of the European social structure. However, it soon became clear the curiosity I felt for everyone I met – an unquenchable inquisitiveness that had me mulling over their voices, their clothes, their habits, the essence that oiled the ticking of their emotional mechanisms – was not reciprocated. My voice put me in a box labeled 'British' where I was ascribed certain virtues and vices. A decent chunk of the people I met returned the compliment of my curiosity, but for general purposes I felt like a faceless immigrant with 'house-trained' stamped across my forehead.

On the other hand, amid a nation seeded with signs for

Serta Mattresses, Dunkin' Donuts, Sir Speedy Photocopies and Meineke Mufflers, I found many Americans were finding ways to signal different brands of humanity. In their fund-raising drives, National Public Radio regularly and unabashedly informs people they will receive free T-shirts or sweatshirts that 'will tell other people that you support NPR'. People treasure meaningful T-shirts, ones that act as flags to attract others of similar castes. No matter how aloof and exclusive one is trying to appear, it is always OK to remark on someone's T-shirt.

'Oh, I see you were at the Nature Conservancy in the Adirondacks! We were just there last week. What did you think?'

My husband, Scott, told me once he believed that, more than acting as social networks, many church organizations existed in the US to create a group to whom it was safe and acceptable to be generous and Christian. In other words, many people felt too insecure to do good to just anyone who needed a hand, so they formed clubs whose members had been preselected. This was a world in which every person, every concept, had to be predigested by someone else before it could be engaged. But, despite the fact I could not feel my new life cohesively through the language of America, the States gave me lots of opportunity to study the quirks of everyday speech. I was thrilled by the fact there are forms of the plural 'you' built into American English in several key areas. For example, in New Jersey, people said 'youse' or 'youse guys' when addressing more than one person, and Pittsburghers have their 'yinz' or 'you-uns'. Although these forms are generally considered substandard, the southern 'y'all' is accepted at all levels of social and formal intercourse. It's as if the immigrants missed a key element of their speech and dragged it back into English, damning the torpedoes as they did so. New expressions were being invented every day for all kinds of situations, many of them joyously lewd.

Living in the midst of this communal linguistic flux was like watching a series of inexorable tides that would whisk up from the sandy beach of everyday life any item no longer of use for the day's transactions, flinging behind some intriguing new object dripping with the shiny wetness of promise and leaving no sediment or memory. 'Palimony' is such a word, a term that gives us a needed new meaning, but whose creation obeys rules of etymology composed by a blithe spirit, not by the ponderous heave-hos of linguistic logic. My own language also underwent a change. The precision of my standard British accent began to erode, and a certain more pliant rhythm wheedled around its corners. I started referring to 'sidewalks', 'kitty cats' and 'cookies' instead of 'pavements', 'pussy cats' and 'biscuits'. The word 'child' began to seem too formal, and I embraced words I would never have dreamed of acknowledging, such as 'shakedown' and 'meltdown'. I did nothing to stop this creeping change, happy to let wordy nature take its course. But, just as I thought I had begun to pass unnoticed, somebody would say something that revealed they hadn't noticed all the Americanisms I'd adopted, only those 'quaint' Briticisms that had yet to fall away. My Spanish went through a similar change. Until that moment, I had spoken a highly sociable form of Castilian with a Galician lilt, eschewing the whiplashing gutturals of the standard language, but retaining everything else. I noticed in academia a completely different type of Spanish was being spoken: a sanitized Pan-Latin American language aimed mainly at US undergraduates and scholars whose native tongue was English. This bowdlerized version of Spanish employed only such vocabulary as may have been acquired in a classroom and avoided any and all natural constructions that did not generally appear in a standard how-to-speak textbook. Very few proverbs or idioms were employed unless they were from the lists periodically fed to undergraduates to learn for tests. No earthy language was ever employed, even between flapping finger-quotes. The language was gutted of all its charm, like a frozen fish on supermarket ice whose taste and smell are impossible to ascertain. Those studying writers from the Iberian Peninsula made certain to use the Castilian lisping theta, which was, given the standardization of codes in progress, just about the only way they could be linguistically distinguished from those interested in Latin American authors. I personally kept up with the theta for years until I realized the vast majority of my students would probably have more dealings with Latin America than with Spain, as I myself did, and, when I finally married into a Cuban American family, I dropped the theta altogether as I was never to hear it within my domestic circle again.

When I married Scott Corrales in 1988, I was able to wet my feet a little more in naturally spoken Spanish. His parents lived at that time in Puerto Rico, whose brand of Spanish differs from that of their native Cuba in its sounds and much of its vocabulary. The family normally spoke English in the house, except to Scott's *abuela*, who, at eighty years of age, was invariably addressed in Spanish because she had forgotten most of her English years before. Apart from this, Scott himself had never used Spanish in the house while growing up because his parents, who spoke excellent, accented English, had wanted him and his elder brother to be mainstream English speakers. Nevertheless, in view of the poor quality of the local schools, they had sent their boys abroad to be educated: Scott to Mexico City and later San Juan, his brother to some aunts in Havana.

One evening not long before Scott and I were married, we were getting ready to go out to dinner for me to meet his father for the first time. As I chose the dress I was going to wear – something dashing but not too unusual had been my main idea – I wondered whether I should address the old gentleman in Spanish or English.

'Doesn't matter,' said Scott happily. 'He speaks both.'

'Yes, I *know* he speaks both,' I answered somewhat impatiently. 'What I want to know is which would he prefer?'

'Ah, well, that's up to you,' replied Scott helpfully, knotting his tie.

This was not as easy a decision as Scott was indicating, and he knew it. On the way to the restaurant in Somerville where we had arranged to meet, my mind raced through the possibilities. I was a native English speaker, and we were in America. I had been told that Mr Corrales spoke English very fluently, if somewhat idiosyncratically, and did so all the time, at nineteen to the dozen. However, it might be a helpfully filial gesture on my part, as a future daughter-in-law and a scholar of Spanish language and literature, if I initiated the conversation in Spanish. Then again, many a well-meaning American has blundered into the quagmire of 'practicing their Spanish' on new Hispanic acquaintances. It can be taken as a patronizing act, as if one were saying, 'I know your English isn't all that good, you uneducated immigrant, you, so let me speak to you in *your* language.' Not a good start when entering a new family!

By the time we got to Somerville, I knew exactly what to do. I would smile and kiss him on the cheek in the politely affectionate manner considered correct for young women and wait to see what his first words would be. I would then follow suit.

Bert Corrales turned out to be a vivacious, smiling man of medium height with black ink pools for eyes and a nose that looked like a model for a Punch-and-Judy show. He could have been a Spaniard, but was clearly much too nattily dressed and, yes, manicured for that. '*¡Hola, m'ija!*' he said, grinning from ear to ear. '*¿Cómo estás?*' We had a wonderful evening together.

Scott told me on the way home that had been the first time he and his father had ever spoken Spanish to each other and it had been quite an experience for the two of them. I was flabbergasted. It had taken an immigrant student from a totally different land to bring that highly significant event about. It was clear that language was a slippery commodity in this new terrain.

I had by now lost faith in my long held credo about the power of language to seduce men. In fact, if I had relied upon it to bring Scott and myself into each other's arms, we would never have passed from constantly jabbering buddies into lovers in the accepted sense. That crucial transition came about one August night as we sat shooting the breeze in my apartment in the Spanish House.

'So how did your vacation in San Juan go?' I asked him, pushing away an overenthusiastic, hairy dog trying to jump on his lap. 'I bet it was great!'

'Well, actually,' Scott began glumly, countermanding my efforts by encouraging the dog to come back for a head-scratch, 'it was a real bust.'

'Oh, no! Why was that?'

'All my friends are no longer there. Some have gotten married, some have moved Stateside... I just realized that I didn't belong there anymore... it just isn't home now.'

This was sickening news indeed. Like me, Scott had been raised in several different parts of the world and, like me, I knew he suffered a deep-seated longing for an anchor. I myself had just come back from a desperately disappointing vacation in Santiago, which I had taken for all the usual reasons, but also to see if a certain friend would finally fall in love with me. He hadn't. Worse than that, I had realized with a clarity that felt more like a death blow that Santiago did not need my attachment or require me to yearn for it. The city that had nourished me for so long at its granite breast was happy to see me finally weaned and on my way. It was managing just fine without its favorite pilgrim.

One glance at Scott's face as he fought back his own disappointment told me in a split second we were alike in ways that transcended language, culture or anything else and, as I threw my arms around his neck, I knew I needed him – all of him – to be part of me in every way. After a couple of months of hesitation on my part regarding the possibility of becoming a spouse, we got married in a colorful ceremony in which every member of the Spanish House was a key participant.

However, the slithery herring of language was still to be my daily bread and, when Scott and I moved to Pittsburgh with his job and then, three years later, left for me to join the faculty at the University of Pittsburgh at Bradford, I was employed once more as its purveyor. To be allowed to do this in the American academic system involved a process as slow and arduous as the trials of Sisyphus carried out on crutches, with one arm in a cast. My thesis two thirds completed after one false start, I was hired at Pitt-Bradford as an Assistant Professor of Spanish, non-tenure track, on the understanding that, if I did not successfully defend my doctoral dissertation within the year, I would be fired. If I was successful, however, I would be taken on as a tenure-track faculty member, one of a group who could aspire to a permanent position after five years at the institution and a thorough examination involving several levels of scrutiny of all my work to date. Saddled with four courses in an unknown working environment and burdened with the effects of an as yet undiagnosed case of diabetes, I labored day and night to teach my classes, get to know all my new colleagues, serve on various ever more exotic committees, do community service in the form of lectures and event-driven presentations and plunge away at the thesis in every remaining moment. Scott refers to this as my 'teach-and-type' period, but it has continued ever since, first in the name of the thesis, then to complete the research and translation projects necessary for tenure and later for the sake of personal survival. It was an exhausting life, particularly because, as a new arrival from Europe during that pre-Internet, pre-postmodern time and despite the presence of several tenured professors better versed in these matters, I was often asked to give lectures on subjects such as world view, styles of conducting business in other cultures, foreign films, love poetry, cuisine – an impromptu expert (only in America!) on the rest of the world. As the years passed, our students became more sophisticated, more aware of world trends, and post-colonialism became a subject to be taught by trendy new faculty members, some of whom were actually post-colonials themselves. As the campus was being sucked slowly into the global village, I was getting older. I achieved tenure and later, very unexpectedly given my dislike of the world of administration, the chair of the Humanities Division – all, it seemed to me, from successfully imitating a drone in the academic honeycomb of language and culture. I made some very close friends and a host of collegial acquaintances and, from the salt mines of life in a small college buried in the forests of the Allegheny Mountains, I began to feel one with my colleagues, a contributor to the life of our community. Suddenly I didn't give a damn about what I or anybody else spoke. I had blended in, a brightly colored, if slightly rickety chair in the firehall of the liberal arts.

    Luckily the potential for the hysterical glee of comedic language was constantly evoked at home, where Scott's translation company and Fortean research projects brought him into contact with a wide variety of folks from all over Spain and Latin America. At school, I limited myself to an example or two of verbal madness in each of my classes. It was a compromise – a tiny dose of linguistic helium in exchange for a growing sense of place.

The month of May 2003 marked a turning point in my acceptance of my hard earned reality. Scott and I had returned from a short trip to New Orleans, where we had been able to bathe in history, unabashed. We had spent three days walking the streets of the French Quarter, sopping up the clear, intricately interwoven layers of Spanish, French, African and shreds of a thousand other contributions to the city's heyday, as well as its more recently flourishing commercial denizens beyond the undrawn line on Canal Street. I had shown Scott the stamping grounds of past literary meetings, the golden glow of the lobby of the dignified Hotel Monteleone, where I had stayed at conferences, the opulent antique stores where every item oozed decadence and craft in equal measure, the anarchical shelves of the voodoo shops, the peculiar scent of streets in the early morning being swabbed of the signs of the previous day's human passers-by, the true, devil-may-care dash and elegance of the clothes in the women's boutiques, and the Bottom of the Cup tea shop on Chartres Street, where seventeen years earlier a sprightly, motherly lady called Connie had foretold I would marry a man in 1988 whose name would be Scott, he would be American and Hispanic, a writer and several years younger than myself. She also told me a number of other things that came true and still are, but I will not mention here for fear of jinxing a good thing. I remembered being delighted to hear all this, but a little surprised my future spouse would not be a *galego* from Santiago.

Despite its many widely publicized tours highlighting every aspect of the city's history, we had come away with the clear impression New Orleans had never betrayed its history, never bowdlerized a single fact, sight or smell of its past. I felt that New Orleans had redeemed the nation's history in some respects by refusing to render any part of itself as quaint, charming or – God forbid! – cute, something I had seen at so many other historical sites. I saw no eerie re-enactments, like that of an excellent and linguistically savvy actor dressed as Benjamin Franklin under his mulberry tree in Philadelphia, trying to make history come alive for the tourist. In New Orleans, you knew you were yourself part of the history, a droplet of water in the river of time nourishing its way through the city. I had always thought of the city as a spa for the soul, especially in the arid early days of the academic desert. For Scott, the reminders of its political and military history provided a constant backdrop of mentally ringing bells and flashbacks of old maps, all of which complemented his memories of the Old San Juan of his youth, where we spent many of our early vacations as a couple. We came home to Pennsylvania, restored in countless ways.

One afternoon, a few days after our return in late May, I was sitting at my desk at school, sorting out the many varied papers that had accumulated since the term had begun to hurtle toward its frantic end, when the phone rang. I put out a desultory hand to answer it.

'Carys Evans-Corrales,' I said in encouraging tones.

'Is that Carys?' asked a determined, but gentle male voice.

'Yes, who's speaking?' I replied. But I already knew before the caller had a chance to answer.

'This is David,' he announced modestly.

I don't know why I didn't acknowledge him immediately. Perhaps I wanted to put that faraway piece of my life through its paces for having taken so long to find me again, so I said in the faux world-weary tones of the teacher with a million students named Dave, 'I'm sorry, David *who*?'

'David Robert,' he replied baldly and so unnecessarily I could have kicked myself for asking.

The conversation that followed, full of joy and curiosity, brought back my youth to me, planting it before me like a gift wrapped in shining paper. David explained he was calling from Jakarta, where his family was now living. My name had come up in a casual conversation and he had subsequently looked me up on the Internet. There he had found me and my vita as part of the faculty information section of the University of Pittsburgh at Bradford's website, complete with phone number, and taken it from there.

I didn't have to tell him much about what I'd been doing all these years, he already knew the general outline. He assumed I had acquired the Corrales part of my name through marriage to someone I'd met during my career as a Hispanist and, of course, he was right. He brought me up to date on the general sweep of his life. He also told me exciting news of what had become of his siblings and other friends of mine from Kuala Lumpur. He appeared to have made a distinguished career for himself and was married to his second wife. He sounded extremely happy, both in his private life and for having found me again after over thirty years. He gave me his email address, and we have been in touch ever since.

'You always said you'd write me into a book,' David reminisced during that phone call. 'And now it turns out that you have!'

'Did I say that?' I asked curiously. Had I really aspired to be a writer that long, a writer without a clear idea of what I was going to say? Here was the proof. And had I known then what role Malaysia was to play in my life?

No, at that point I didn't know it myself. The first chapter of this book had been left pretty much as it was before that phone call. But it was the photograph David sent me immediately afterwards that is the centerpiece of this particularly glowing table of coalescing, elemental dreams. It was taken a few days earlier, at a celebration after his son's graduation from a well-known secondary institution in Singapore, and depicted, as one might expect, a joyful family marking an important life event. On the left is the proud, middle-aged father, on the right his elegant wife, between them an intensely handsome youth in a dark suit and glittering, copper-colored vest, a slightly younger, very postmodern fellow in dreadlocks and, keeping close to his mother's skirts, the baby of the family, a five-year-old boy looking like an ad for gorgeous childhood. I was surprised to find that David was by no means the focus of my interest. Somehow, despite the years and a clear acquisition of fatherly gravitas, he looked just the same as my memory of him. I found myself absorbed by how *exotic* David's family looked, how different from the people I remembered in Kuala Lumpur.

This sense of foreignness – caused not entirely by the fact this seemed to be an Indonesian, not a Malaysian, family – has been the spell that has brought down the walled fortress that for so long prevented my embracing of the past. They *are* foreign. I can go and visit and not feel like a Malaysian girl manqué, a clumsy, former expat come to drag back a past Southeast Asia has already forgotten. Gone is any lingering sense of British-imposed restraint, gone is everything from anywhere this family doesn't want to hear of. Present is everything this family wants to embrace. The lands of my youth have taken off behind my back and forgotten me, soaring off into their dreams, alighting on earth of their choosing. If I return, I shall be thrilled to be a tourist, marveling among the newness of what I had almost lost forever.

ALSO AVAILABLE FROM SMALL STATIONS PRESS

Rosalía de Castro, GALICIAN SONGS
Translated by Erín Moure

Rosalía de Castro (1837-1885) is considered the founder of modern Galician literature. She wrote three major books of poetry: two in Galician, *Galician Songs* and *New Leaves*, and one in Spanish, *On the Banks of the Sar*. Nourished by the popular songs the author heard around her, *Galician Songs* was first published in 1863 and dedicated on 17 May, the date that a hundred years later, in 1963, would become and has remained Galician Literature Day, when the work of a particular Galician author is celebrated. *Galician Songs* marks the first full publication of any of Rosalía de Castro's books of poetry in English and is accompanied by a translator's introduction that argues for the importance and contemporaneity of the author's work and poetics, not just in Galician, but in English.

Pilar Pallarés, A LEOPARD AM I
Translated by Carys Evans-Corrales

Pilar Pallarés is considered one of the most evocative voices in contemporary Galician poetry. *A Leopard Am I*, published in Galician in 2011, is her fourth poetry collection and was awarded the poetry prize of the Galician-Language Writers Association. She has also published *In the Dusk* (1980), *Seventh Solitude* (1984, winner of the Esquío Prize for poetry) and *Book of Devorations* (1996, winner of the Galician Critics' Prize for literary creation). She has written extensively on other Galician poets such as Rosalía de Castro, Luís Pimentel and Ricardo Carvalho Calero. This is her first collection to appear in English.

Jonathan Dunne, THE LIFE OF A TRANSLATOR

How are English words connected? Is there a consistent set of rules by which words in the English language are connected not according to their etymology, their evolution over time, but according to their letters? These letters may be rearranged, read back to front, altered according to the laws of phonetics, their position in the alphabet, their physical appearance, their numerical value. So while the reverse of **live** is **evil**, we can count down from I to O and find **love** instead (as **sin** gives **son**). The **ego**, by taking a step back in the alphabet, can be turned into **God**. Using the laws of phonetics, we can realize that the true purpose of the **self** is to **serve**. In *The Life of a Translator*, Jonathan Dunne offers a clear, direct introduction to the ways in which English words can be connected according to their DNA, arguing that words have something to tell us about human life, but their meaning is hidden and must be deciphered (**God** is **code**). In this sense, language is similar to the environment. We think we see what is around us, but we are spiritually blind even after we have opened our eyes, and it is this spiritual blindness causing a crisis in the world because of how we treat our world, the environment, each other and, ultimately, ourselves.

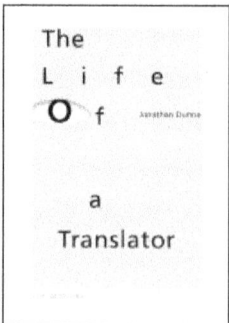

For an up-to-date list of our publications, please visit our website
www.smallstations.com

www.ingramcontent.com/pod-product-compliance
Lightning Source LLC
Chambersburg PA
CBHW031956080426
42735CB00007B/412